T0302065

Global Perspectives on Frameworks for Integrated Reporting:

Emerging Research and Opportunities

Ioana Dragu
Babes-Bolyai University, Romania

Adriana Tiron-Tudor
Babes-Bolyai University, Romania

Szilveszter Fekete Pali-Pista
Babes-Bolyai University, Romania

A volume in the Advances in Web
Technologies and Engineering
(AWTE) Book Series

Published in the United States of America by
   IGI Global
   Business Science Reference (an imprint of IGI Global)
   701 E. Chocolate Avenue
   Hershey PA, USA 17033
   Tel: 717-533-8845
   Fax: 717-533-8661
   E-mail: cust@igi-global.com
   Web site: http://www.igi-global.com

Library of Congress Cataloging-in-Publication Data

Names: Dragu, Ioana, 1987- author. | Tiron-Tudor, Adriana, 1968- author. |
   Fekete Pali-Pista, Szilveszter, 1978- author.
Title: Global perspectives on frameworks for integrated reporting : emerging
   research and opportunities / by Ioana Dragu, Adriana Tiron-Tudor, and
   Szilveszter Fekete Pali-Pista.
Description: Hershey : Business Science Reference, [2017]
Identifiers: LCCN 2017010688| ISBN 9781522527534 (hardcover) | ISBN
   9781522527541 (ebook)
Subjects: LCSH: Auditors' reports.
Classification: LCC HF5667.6 .D73 2017 | DDC 657.3--dc23 LC record available at https://lccn.
loc.gov/2017010688

This book is published in the IGI Global book series Advances in Web Technologies and Engineering (AWTE) (ISSN: 2328-2762; eISSN: 2328-2754)

British Cataloguing in Publication Data
A Cataloguing in Publication record for this book is available from the British Library.

For electronic access to this publication, please contact: eresources@igi-global.com.

Advances in Web Technologies and Engineering (AWTE) Book Series

ISSN:2328-2762
EISSN:2328-2754

Editor-in-Chief: Ghazi I. Alkhatib, The Hashemite University, Jordan & David C. Rine, George Mason University, USA

MISSION

The **Advances in Web Technologies and Engineering (AWTE) Book** Series aims to provide a platform for research in the area of Information Technology (IT) concepts, tools, methodologies, and ethnography, in the contexts of global communication systems and Web engineered applications. Organizations are continuously overwhelmed by a variety of new information technologies, many are Web based. These new technologies are capitalizing on the widespread use of network and communication technologies for seamless integration of various issues in information and knowledge sharing within and among organizations. This emphasis on integrated approaches is unique to this book series and dictates cross platform and multidisciplinary strategy to research and practice.

The **Advances in Web Technologies and Engineering (AWTE) Book Series** seeks to create a stage where comprehensive publications are distributed for the objective of bettering and expanding the field of web systems, knowledge capture, and communication technologies. The series will provide researchers and practitioners with solutions for improving how technology is utilized for the purpose of a growing awareness of the importance of web applications and engineering.

COVERAGE

- Case studies validating Web-based IT solutions
- Human factors and cultural impact of IT-based systems
- Quality of service and service level agreement issues among integrated systems
- Software agent-based applications
- IT education and training
- Security, integrity, privacy, and policy issues
- Mobile, location-aware, and ubiquitous computing
- Strategies for linking business needs and IT
- IT readiness and technology transfer studies
- Web systems engineering design

IGI Global is currently accepting manuscripts for publication within this series. To submit a proposal for a volume in this series, please contact our Acquisition Editors at Acquisitions@igi-global.com or visit: http://www.igi-global.com/publish/.

Titles in this Series

For a list of additional titles in this series, please visit:
https://www.igi-global.com/book-series/advances-web-technologies-engineering/37158

Novel Design and the Applications of Smart-M3 Platform in the Internet of Things ...
Dmitry Korzun (Petrozavodsk State University (PetrSU), Russia) Alexey Kashevnik (St. Petersburg Institute for Informatics and Automation of the Russian Academy of Sciences (SPIIRAS), Russia & ITMO University, Russia) and Sergey Balandin (FRUCT Oy, Finland & St. Petersburg State University of Aerospace Instrumentation (SUAI) Russia)
Information Science Reference • ©2018 • 150pp • H/C (ISBN: 9781522526537) • US $145.00

Developing Metadata Application Profiles
Mariana Curado Malta (Polytechnic of Oporto, Portugal & Algoritmi Center, University of Minho, Portugal) Ana Alice Baptista (Algoritmi Center, University of Minho, Portugal) and Paul Walk (University of Edinbrgh, UK)
Information Science Reference • ©2017 • 248pp • H/C (ISBN: 9781522522218) • US $170.00

Game Theory Solutions for the Internet of Things Emerging Research and Opportunities
Sungwook Kim (Sogang University, South Korea)
Information Science Reference • ©2017 • 221pp • H/C (ISBN: 9781522519522) • US $130.00

Design Solutions for Improving Website Quality and Effectiveness
G. Sreedhar (Rashtriya Sanskrit Vidyapeetha (Deemed University), India)
Information Science Reference • ©2016 • 423pp • H/C (ISBN: 9781466697645) • US $220.00

Handbook of Research on Redesigning the Future of Internet Architectures
Mohamed Boucadair (France Télécom, France) and Christian Jacquenet (France Télécom, France)
Information Science Reference • ©2015 • 621pp • H/C (ISBN: 9781466683716) • US $345.00

Artificial Intelligence Technologies and the Evolution of Web 3.0
Tomayess Issa (Curtin University, Australia) and Pedro Isaías (Universidade Aberta (Portuguese Open University), Portugal)
Information Science Reference • ©2015 • 422pp • H/C (ISBN: 9781466681477) • US $225.00

For an enitre list of titles in this series, please visit:
https://www.igi-global.com/book-series/advances-web-technologies-engineering/37158

701 East Chocolate Avenue, Hershey, PA 17033, USA
Tel: 717-533-8845 x100 • Fax: 717-533-8661
E-Mail: cust@igi-global.com • www.igi-global.com

Table of Contents

Preface

This book discusses the challenges of integrated reporting (IR), a relative new reporting scheme that assumes the disclosure of both financial and non-financial information in a single, unified corporate report. With the objective of defining a prototype framework for integrated reports, we addressed in the first place the accountancy profession, the main authority in corporate reporting field. Then, obtaining relevant opinions from specialists, tax advisors, auditors, accountants, practitioners, or other members of accountancy profession, we were in the position of setting the main coordinates for our IR Framework. The final step was to test our prototype framework on a sample of approximately 500 global corporations. The purpose of this research was to investigate the level of IR absorption within the corporate business environment, based on our IR elements resulted from accountancy profession expertise, International Integrated Reporting Committee (IIRC) Guidelines, IFRS standards with impact on both financial and non-financial information, social audit standards, or disclosure requirements set up by a Directive of the European Union.

The first chapter of this book makes a trespassing through the most relevant (and recent) literature review in the fields of integrated reporting, corporate disclosure, accounting theories etc. This section aims to present previous studies on our topic. The second chapter outlines the methodologies used in our research, in the same time explaining the necessity of preparing the questionnaire/ survey for accountancy profession members, and the other stages of research, setting up the IR Framework based on the relevant items, using the disclosure software for gathering the information, data modeling, SPSS processing. Chapter three presents on a step-by-step basis how we arrived at our conceptual model of integrated report (the Framework). In chapter four, we discuss the obtained results, engaging in a rough and detailed analysis.

This book seeks to serve a large category of audience, mainly grouped into preparers and users of corporate reports: multinational companies, business environment, analysts, accountants, auditors, managers, professional organizations, academic environment, researchers, etc.

Introduction

BACKGROUND ON INTEGRATED REPORTING <IR> FRAMEWORK DEVELOPMENT

Our vision of *Integrated Reporting <IR> Framework* involves an evolution from voluntary requirements of the International Integrated Reporting Council, to general guidelines issued at European level (by the European Commission: EC, Federation of European Accountants: FEE), or at global scale (International Federation of Accountants: IFAC). The first sign of regulation in the field of non-financial information is attributed to the United Nations that issued a document on legal and practical aspects of Environmental, Social and Governance (ESG) information. The final stage in the evolution of IR should emerge in changing the nature of information from voluntary to mandatory that can be achieved when the main authority in the accountancy field – International Accounting Standards Board (IASB)/ international Financial Reporting Standards (IFRS) issues a global standard for integrated reporting. The IASB/IFRS have to align to current corporate reporting trends and join efforts with other professional bodies to contribute to the development of integrated reports.

We define an original framework for Integrated Reporting, from the voluntary initiatives of the IIRC- International Integrated Reporting Council, European Union (EU) Directives, to the mandatory IASB-IFRS. Our *conceptual model* contains the following items:

- Content elements and principles issued by the IIRC (reviewed after the viewpoints expressed by Institute of Chartered Accountants in England and Wales: ICAEW, IFAC, FEE, and other accounting organizations)
- Disclosure rules from IFRS-IASB accounting standards with direct impact on IR

- Non- financial information disclosure norms in terms of the European Commission initiatives
- SA8000 and AA1000 social audit standards and their influence on annual reports

In developing the conceptual model of integrated reporting, we started from the IIRC Content Elements and Principles listed in the Final Framework published by Council on December 2013.

However, the IIRC focuses more on the non- financial sphere, and little attention is given to the financial (and accounting) side. We consider that accountancy profession has a major role in the evolution of integrated reporting by providing guidance for the application of integrated reporting, and even issuing standards/ regulation for this field. Thus, our model aims to show the impact of IFRS/IASB international accounting standards on integrated reporting by finding common elements between standards' requirements regarding the information disclosed in annual reports and the social and environmental performance outlined by the IIRC.

During this book we develop a disclosure index for measuring the level or IR. This 'integration scale' (that also stands for an original *prototype framework*) was built starting from IIRC framework and the comments received from international organizations and members of accountancy profession. The main purpose was to find the main IR determinants from an international perspective. We have tested the prototype framework on 600 corporations, models of best corporate citizenship. Data gathering was done using Tropes semantic software, while data analysis and interpretation involved SPSS computation and testing. Only 485 companies from the total sample had available reports in all the years of analysis. Therefore, we continued with the statistical study for these corporations, still including more than 2.000 observations (annual reports from our sample in all the five years). After applying several tests in SPSS, we found that IR registers significant evolutions in time- from a year to another. Another conclusion was that the diversity of companies generated different reporting behaviors, as we obtained significant discrepancies in the level of DI, with some exceptions in which the degree of IR was similar between companies in a certain year. Regarding the final stage of the research, we identified the following factors with a relevant statistical impact on the disclosure of IR information: number of employees, total assets, market capitalization, industry (as organizational characteristics, accounting standards), GDP, HDI, legal system (as country- level indicators).

All the aspects mentioned above have been validated through various statistical techniques. We also formulate more hypothesis that have been tested using the previous techniques. Finally, the study brings an important contribution to corporate reporting literature, through its original approach, being the first research that develops a conceptual framework for integrated reporting with the purpose of determining the disclosure level for the elements included in the framework and to establish an integration scale. More than that, the book managed to define a set of impact factors for IR, therefore investigates the causality effect in relation to integrated reporting.

The current manuscript is addressed to academics, scholars, students, PhD candidates, post-doctoral candidates, practitioners, accountants, experts, auditors, regulators, corporate environment, analysis, investors, creditors etc., or any other person interested in reporting, accounting, disclosure of financial and non-financial information, data analysis, or business and economics fields in general.

INTRODUCTION

One cannot ask for the same 'information disclosure package' from a pharmaceutical corporation compared to a firm in the food industry. At the same time, banks have less impact on the environment when compared with companies operating in the oil and gas sector. Further on, the larger the company is, the greater the volume of information disclosed. Thus, the size (measured by total assets or number of employees) is another important parameter. In addition, reporting patterns change with company sector, size, profitability, attitude towards debt, investor behavior, etc. The same applies for the external economic conditions- measured by Gross Domestic Product (GDP), stock exchange influence (as market capitalization), political pressure (civil/common law countries), or even the general social responsibility attitude (NCRI, HDI, CPI).

This book contains *two main research sections*: the first one refers to the development of a survey addressed to accountancy profession, which had the purpose to investigate the type of information to be included in the integrated report or the structure of the IR. The second study involves a sample of 437 companies[1] and a five- year's period of analysis. We try to identify whether the reports issued by the organizations from our sample comply with our model of integrated reporting. The first stage was to construct a disclosure index for measuring the level of integrated reporting information in the annual reports.

We argue that this framework is relevant because its elements are based on previous research and they were interpreted according to international accounting standards (IFRS/IASB, respectively IFRIC: International Financial Reporting Interpretations Committee). In addition, the model contains determinants (at organizational and country levels) that have been previously tested in the international literature in correlation with sustainability/ CSR/ integrated reporting schemes.

ENDNOTE

[1]   From the initial sample of approximately 600 organizations, only 437 had annual reports available in all the years included in the analysis (2009-2010-2011-2012-2013).

Chapter 1
Literature Review

ABSTRACT

Within the current chapter, we present the most relevant (and recent) literature review in the fields of integrated reporting, corporate disclosure, accounting theories, etc. This section incorporates previous studies on our topic. We explain the integrated reporting (IR) origins from corporate social responsibility (CSR) and sustainability perspectives. In addition, we set the coordinates for the 'integration' process as new disclosure mechanism of corporate reports, in the form of economic, social, and financial mix integration. Finally, the chapter deepens the understanding upon corporate reporting theories that can explain the integrated reporting trend: institutional theory, legitimacy theory and positive accounting theory.

INTRODUCTION

Previous studies in the IR field make reference to the non-financial information from the European Directive requirements (Janek et al., 2016), or the paradigms of financial, social, and economic integration (Barker & Kasim, 2016, Dumay et al., 2016; de Villiers et al., 2014; Perego et al., 2016). Further on, scholars and academics underline the relevance of social investors (Adams et al., 2016) or firm valuation in the context of IR (Lee & Yeo, 2016). Further on, there has been a strong interest for the research on IR frameworks (Cheng et al., 2014; Abeysekera, 2013). What defines this book as a relevant contributor to corporate reporting, in general, and IR in particular, is the fact that, in addition to what other scholars investigated, we present an accumulation

DOI: 10.4018/978-1-5225-2753-4.ch001

of theories, methods, and studies, that convey practical insights. This is the first work that seeks to determine what information should be included in an integrated report, how this information has to be organized and structured, and how can companies adopt IR more efficiently. Only accountancy profession could provide relevant answers to these questions, so we set up a survey study targeting the accountancy environment: accountants, experts, auditors, professionals, academics, etc. Their answered served for the second part of our investigation, in which we develop a framework prototype for IR and we test this framework internationally, on a large sample of companies. Thus, this is the first work covering such an extensive and original study on IR, in which we use a software for measuring the disclosure level in companies' corporate reports.

As integrated reporting has evolved from sustainability (Janek et al., 2016) and CSR reporting, we can deduce that it incorporates some common elements. Thereof, IR should depend on the same organizational characteristics as CSR and sustainability, such as size and profitability of the company, activity area, as well as on national, or country-level indicators (Gray et al., 1995; Artiachet al., 2010). In addition, country-level indicator, such as HDI, CPI, and BPI (Vaiman et al., 2011; Cornachione et al., 2008; Lee & Carter, 2011; Jensen & Berg, 2012), as well as the country origin of law (Dragu & Tudor-Tiron, 2014; Jensen & Berg, 2012), or GDP (Jensen & Berg, 2012), and not least market capitalization (Jamali et al., 2008), are often correlated with sustainability and CSR disclosure in corporate literature.

Both institutional theory and legitimacy theory show presumption of certain impact that external factors have on corporate disclosure. Further on, the political factors (represented by the variables of country and law of origin) can represent the coercive side of the institutional theory and be completed by the legitimate of the state, or legitimacy theory (Jensen & Berg, 2011). There are other indicators that maintain external influence on the organizations and the level of disclosure from their annual reports. CPI (Corruption Perception Index) is a national level indicator ranking the states according to the degree of corruption from the public sector[1].

The introduction of financial indicators in our model as influencing variables is based on the positive accounting theory (Guidry & Patten, 2012; Ohlson, 1980; Setyorini & Ishak, 2012). This relates to one of the principles stipulated in the PAT- positive accounting theory that suggests non-financial disclosure means increase in firm performance and profitability, and automatically- high bonuses for managers (Banwarie, 2011; Robert, 1992; Chan, 2003; Barako et al., 2006; Haniffa & Cooke, 2005; Willekens et al., 2005). Analogical, the total assets and market capitalization also derive from positive accounting theory, as elements of financial performance and profitability (Banwarie, 2011; Robert, 1992; Chan, 2003; Barako et al., 2006; Haniffa & Cooke, 2005; Willekens et al., 2005; Setyorini & Ishak, 2012).

Our research framework contributes to the development of a proper econometric model that shows the association between the dependent variable-IR, and the independent ones: country, industry, total assets, number of employees, market value, price per share, debt to equity, operating income, market capitalization, law of origin, HDI, GDP, CPI (Figure no. 5).

REFERENCES

Abeysekera, I. (2013). A template for integrated reporting. *Journal of Intellectual Capital, 14*(2), 227–245.

Adams, C. A., Potter, B., Singh, P. J., & York, J. (2016). Exploring the implications of integrated reporting for social investment (disclosures). *The British Accounting Review, 48*(3), 283–296.

Banwarie, U. R. (2011). *The relationship between ownership structure and CSR disclosure* (Unpublished doctoral thesis). Erasmus National University, Rotterdam, The Netherlands.

Barker, R., & Kasim, T. (2016). Integrated reporting: Precursor of a paradigm shift in corporate reporting?. In Integrated reporting (pp. 81-108). Palgrave Macmillan UK.

Cheng, M., Green, W., Conradie, P., Konishi, N., & Romi, A. (2014). The international integrated reporting framework: Key issues and future research opportunities. *Journal of International Financial Management & Accounting, 25*(1), 90–119. doi:10.1111/jifm.12015

de Villiers, C., Rinaldi, L., & Unerman, J. (2014). Integrated Reporting: Insights, gaps and an agenda for future research. *Accounting, Auditing & Accountability Journal, 27*(7), 1042–1067. doi:10.1108/AAAJ-06-2014-1736

Dragu, I., & Tudor-Tiron, A. (2014). Form Sustainability to Integrated Reporting –The Political Perspective of Institutional Theory. *Studia Universitatis Babes Bolyai-Oeconomica,* (2), 20-33.

Dumay, J., Bernardi, C., Guthrie, J., & Demartini, P. (2016, September). Integrated reporting: A structured literature review. *Accounting Forum, 40*(3), 166–185. doi:10.1016/j.accfor.2016.06.001

Gray, R., Kouhy, R., & Lavers, S. (1995). Corporate social and environmental reporting: A review of the literature and a longitudinal study of UK disclosure. *Accounting, Auditing & Accountability Journal, 8*(2), 47–77. doi:10.1108/09513579510146996

Guidry, R. P., & Patten, D. M. (2012). Voluntary disclosure theory and financial control variables: An assessment of recent environmental disclosure research. *Accounting Forum, 36*(2), 81–90. doi:10.1016/j.accfor.2012.03.002

Jamali, D., Safieddine, A. M., & Rabbath, M. (2008). Corporate governance and corporate social responsibility synergies and interrelationships. *Corporate Governance: An International Review, 16*(5), 443–459. doi:10.1111/j.1467-8683.2008.00702.x

Janek, C., Riccerib, F., Sangiorgia, D., & Guthrie, J. (2016). *Sustainability and integrated reporting: A case study of a large multinational organisation.* Academic Press.

Jensen, C. J., & Berg, N. (2012). Determinants of traditional sustainability reporting versus integrated reporting: An institutionalist approach. *Business Strategy and the Environment, 21*(5), 299–316. doi:10.1002/bse.740

Lee, K. W., & Yeo, G. H. H. (2016). The association between integrated reporting and firm valuation. *Review of Quantitative Finance and Accounting, 47*(4), 1221–1250. doi:10.1007/s11156-015-0536-y

Perego, P., Kennedy, S., & Whiteman, G. (2016). A lot of icing but little cake? Taking integrated reporting forward. *Journal of Cleaner Production, 136*, 53–64. doi:10.1016/j.jclepro.2016.01.106

ENDNOTE

[1]   http://www.transparency.org/research/cpi/overview.

Chapter 2
Research Methodology

ABSTRACT

This chapter clarifies the research methodology adopted for attaining our objective stated previously in this manuscript. The methodology involves two main parts: the development of a survey or questionnaire targeting members of accountancy profession, and the set-up of a prototype framework meant to test the IR adoption in the corporate business environment. We also explain our research questions that represent the fundament for the path of this book. Therefore, we should ask ourselves: What is "integration"? Which information should be included in an integrated report and why? These two questions are answered through the application of the questionnaire and the development and testing of the IR Framework.

INTRODUCTION

The first part of the current research focuses on providing deeper understanding on the meaning of *integrated reporting* and its impact upon stakeholders. We decided to set up a questionnaire addressed to professional accountants, members of professional accounting bodies, who can meet one or more roles from the below list of internal and external stakeholders: employees, managers, owners[1], shareholders, creditors, customers, suppliers, government, and society (Figure 1).

DOI: 10.4018/978-1-5225-2753-4.ch002

Figure 1. Internal and external stakeholders
Source: www.boundless.com

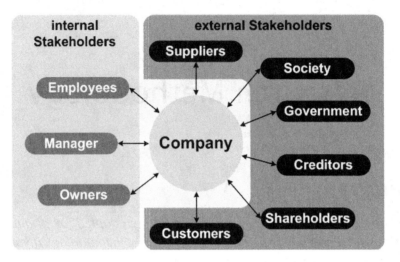

In addition, we mention the stakeholder classification from the IIRC perspective of focus groups: the accounting profession, regulators and standard setters, companies, investors, intergovernmental organizations, civil society and academia[2]. We considered an extended range of stakeholders (adding the category of internal stakeholders to this list), because we aimed to investigate how integrated reporting is assimilated in practice, by people performing different roles in an organization, from accountants, to managers, or company owners, who are also members of accountancy profession. Our questionnaire was sent through e-mail to practitioners and members of accountancy profession. We obtained the e-mail addresses from the sites of international accounting professional bodies and from other internal sources within these organizations. In addition, we also used an interactive online platform on which participants could register and complete the questionnaire. We have sent 97 questionnaires to people from accounting sphere: experts, members of accounting professional bodies, managers, employees. We received feedback responses from 69 accounting professionals, members of international professional bodies. Respondents are affiliated to professional accounting bodies, respectively groups of professional accounting bodies, being ACCA students, members of ACCA, CAFR- The Chamber of Financial Auditors of Romania, CECCAR- The Body of Expert and Licensed Accountants of Romania, ACFE- Association of Certified Fraud Examiners, IIA- The Institute of Internal Auditors. In addition, respondents fulfill one or more roles of an internal/external stakeholder, from employees (accountants, controllers, analysts, experts, tax specialists) to managers (including CFOs as top management, seniors, leaders) or owners (associates/main associates of accounting firms), and from creditors (bank operations specialists) to suppliers of financial services (auditors), or training services (trainers). The main categories of respondents are preparers and users of annual reports, accounting firms and organizations. Before beginning with the first set of questions, we asked people to define the level of their understanding and expertise in the area of integrated reporting as *slight, moderate average, good, or very good*. 32 respondents consider they have a *good* knowledge in the field of integrated reporting, 9 agree of having an *average* level of understanding, while 7 believe they hold *very good* knowledge on IR, 6 asses themselves in as *moderate* level of understanding the area, and only 2 admit they *slightly* heard about IR. 13 people choose not to reply to this question, but still we can deduct an overall good level of knowledge and expertise in our sample of respondents. However, we remarked that the number of those having a good expertise in IR is less than half of our sample (32 out of a total of 69 respondents). At the end of the questionnaire, we included a section for personal suggestions or additional comments one would like to add (see Appendix 4).

Going into more detail, our sample includes 69 respondents, nine are ACCA students, 28 represent ACCA full members, two respondents are part of three professional accounting bodies: ACCA, CAFR, and CECCAR, one is a member of ACFE and IIA. The sample also includes four CECCAR members, two professionals affiliated to IFAC, three persons who have no affiliation, while 20 respondents preferred not to reveal their (possible) affiliation to any accounting professional body. In addition, seven work as accountants, other seven are analysts, four are auditors, one is a banking operation specialist, and we also have one trainer and a single tax specialist. Further on, three CFOs from top management, eleven controllers, two experts, one leader, and ten managers[3] responded to our questionnaire. Out of the total of 69, eight respondents represent accounting firms, other are part of an organization, 24 admit they are preparers of annual reports, seven consider themselves users of annual reports, while the rest find themselves in other categories not mentioned in this questionnaire.

The questionnaire contains 43 questions, out of which 9 are *open* and 34 *closed*. Besides these, we requested the respondents to provide some personal information on education, professional background as well as to argument

Table 1. Description of respondents

Affiliation	Position	Category
ACCA	Accountant	accounting firm
CAFR	Analyst	organization
CECCAR	Auditor	preparer of annual report
ACFE	banking operation specialist	user of annual report
IFAC	CFO	
IIA	Controller	
	Expert	
	junior auditor	
	Leader	
	Manager	
	tax specialist	
	Trainer	

Source: author's design

the answers to certain questions by including additional explanations. In Appendix 2 you can find our questionnaire addressed to the professional accountants. We distributed the questionnaire on three categories of people: academics, practitioners, and members of accounting professional bodies. The feedback received in this initial stage helped us in setting the order of questions in the questionnaire, and adding some general questions to assess the knowledge of the participant in the field of IR, and to encourage them to provide additional comments if case (Questions no. 1 and 43).

The questionnaire was meant to provide an answer for the following research questions:

- What is "integration"?
- Which information should be included in an integrated report and why?

In order to better understand IR, we should start by clarifying what does *integration* mean, as a concept/ process/ reporting behavior. The IIRC (2012) considers that integration can be achieved through an interaction between companies' reports, information categories (financial/ non-financial- social or environmental etc.). Then, the 6 capitals and the value creation process stand at the core of IR. Further on, IR becomes a set of connected elements, from internal and external information, to departments and people within the organization. To summarize, our first research question incorporates more investigation areas, namely:

1. The interaction between the financial and non-financial information; IR versus other reports.
2. The capitals and the value creation process.
3. Defining integrated reporting (connectivity/interconnection/connect internal and external information/departments and people within the organization).

After explaining the true essence of integration, we decided to develop a discussion on what information should be included in an IR framework, and if the benefits of reporting this information in an integrated manner justify the costs of such reporting processes. Also, we are interested in finding which factors influence the disclosure degree presented in an integrated report, in order to explain why would companies adopt and implement IR. We include the industry as a relevant differentiator for the type of information to be included in the integrated report. In addition, we aim to receive recommendations from the respondents regarding the elements and principles from the IIRC Framework, as well as certain IR information characteristics: *relevance* and *materiality*. Finally, we address the voluntary versus mandatory IR debate, with implications on IR assurance. Therefore, the second research question continues with an IR framework discussion cumulating six more areas:

4. IR costs and benefits;
5. Determinants of integrated reporting;
6. Recommendations concerning the IIRC Framework;
7. The industry;
8. Characteristics for IR information;
9. Voluntary versus mandatory IR and assurance.

In the second part of the research, we develop the IR framework prototype. The first step is to build an integration scale, for measuring with the help of a disclosure index, the level of IR information disclosure in companies' annual reports (Figure 2).

Our scale of integration presented above was meant to explain our disclosure checklist. Each sequence of words has been considered for the semantic analysis, using the *Tropes* software, as *Tropes* allows users to develop their own checklists. We downloaded the annual reports issued by the companies

Table 2. Building an integration scale: the IR disclosure index

IIRC	
Content Elements	**Principles**
Mission	Strategic focus
Vision	Future orientation
Strategy	Connectivity of information
Business Model	Stakeholder responsiveness
Performance	Materiality
Governance	Conciseness
Future outlook	Reliability
Opportunities	Completeness
Risks	Consistency
Report preparation	Comparability
Report presentation	
IFRS	
IFRS Impact on Environmental Information	**IFRS Impact on CSR Information**
Intangible assets exploration of mineral resources	Recognition of provision
Emission rights assets	Present obligation
Concessions, licenses, trademarks, and similar items	Outflow of resources
Other intangible assets	Reasonable estimate
Tangible assets	
Tangible assets with exploration of mineral resources	Disclosure on CSR information
Inventories /waste	Commitment to transparency
Environmental provisions	obligation to societies
Emission rights governmental grant	reputation risk
Fines and taxes for environmental purposes	Commitment to investors
Other environmental expenses	
Contingent liabilities and assets	
European Commission	
Proposal for a Directive of the European Parliament and of the Council	
Non-Financial Information	**Diversity**
Environmental information	Age
Social information	Gender
Employee- related information	Geographical diversity

continued on following page

Table 2. Continued

respect of human rights	Educational and professional background
anti-corruption	
Bribery	
Social Audit	
SA 8000	**AA 1000**
Child labour	Inclusivity
Forced labour	Materiality
Compulsory labour	Responsiveness
Health and Safety	Integrate with governance
Freedom of Association	Integrate with organizational strategy and operations management
Right to Collective Bargaining	Purpose of stakeholder engagement
Discrimination	Stakeholder identification
Disciplinary Practices	Profile and map stakeholders
Working Hours	Determine engagement level and method
Remuneration	
Management Systems	

Source: author's design

in our sample during the 5-year period: 2009-2013 (437 companies x 5 years = 2,185 annual reports). Then, each annual report was introduced into software analysis, by a simple *drag and drop* command. The programme generated thousands of excel sheets that contained reports on the disclosure level (measured as frequency) for each item from the DI. The next step was to centralize of all this data in a single or unique database. This database contained all the necessary information (including summary on disclosure index per years, organizational characteristics, and country – level indicators).

We intend to test our framework on approximately 600 global corporations (Appendix 1). The sample has been chosen from various sources, namely: the IIRC Pilot Programme, GRI's G4 Participants, GRI Awards, CRRA Winners Best Report 2012, A4S, Integrated reports from sustainabilityreports.com, Global 100, 100 Best Corporate Citizens, Corporate Responsibility Magazine, Most admired companies, Forbes magazine (March 21, 2011 issue). The corporations quoted in the above databases are believed to be more oriented towards presenting non-financial information in their reports, in addition to the traditional financial data (Wild & van Staden, 2013; Zickiene & Juozaitiene, 2013; Dusek & Fukuda, 2012; Aceituno et al., 2013; Dawkins &

Ngunjiri, 2008; Verschoor & Murphy, 2002; Filbeck & Preece, 1998; Reilly & Hynan, 2014). Using *Tropes semantic software*, we performed a content analysis on these companies' annual reports and check if these comply with our framework on integrated reporting. We have also computed a scorecard that for measuring the *degree of integration* for each company. The scorecard represents the sum of frequencies in the disclosure of each element in our framework.

Further on, we conducted the investigation on the annual reports for the period 2009 - 2013. We have chosen to start with 2009 because this year represents a crossroad in the development of integrated reporting. This was the year when the Republic of South Africa started to implement mandatory integrated reporting (following – The King Code of Governance Principles and the King Report on Governance) and international stock exchanges started to issue requirements for sustainability disclosure that could be useful to investors (TMX Group; NYSE Euronext, BM & FBOVESPA, Bourse de Luxembourg). At the same time, scholars and academics were publishing papers on integrated reporting or related areas (Lozano, 2009; Vidal & Kozak, 2009; Michael, 2009; Nidumolu et al., 2009) and the interest in integrated reporting started to grow within international conferences or workshops (Mammat, 2009). In our opinion, a five-year analysis period conveys a proper perspective on integrated reporting evolution. Thus, we seek to investigate the compliance with the framework as an evolution, in order to observe which elements from the framework are being constantly disclosed and reported on from one year to another.

REFERENCES

Lozano, R. (2009). *Orchestrating Organisational Change for Corporate Sustainability. Strategies to overcome resistance to change and to facilitate institutionalization* (PhD Doctoral thesis). Cardiff University, Cardiff, UK.

Mammat, J. (2009). *Integrated sustainability reporting and assurance.* Paper Presented at CIS Corporate Governance Conference. Retrieved from http://www.ciscorpgov.co.za/present/CIS%20WEBSITE/Mammatt_Integrated%20Sustainability%20Reporting%20and%20Assurance.pdf

Reilly, A. H., & Hynan, K. A. (2014). Corporate communication, sustainability, and social media: Its not easy (really) being green. *Business Horizons, 57*(6), 747–758. doi:10.1016/j.bushor.2014.07.008

Vidal, N. G., & Kozak, R. A. (2009). From forest certification to corporate responsibility: Adapting to changing global competitive factors. *Proceedings of the XIII World Forestry Congress 2009: Forests in Development – A Vital Balance.*

Wild, S., & van Staden, C. J. (2013, July). Integrated reporting: Initial analysis of early reporters–An institutional theory approach. *7th Asia Pacific Interdisciplinary Accounting Research Conference*, 26-28.

Zickiene, S., & Juozaitiene, L. (2013). Disclosure of environmental, social and governance information using diverse reporting schemes. *Social Research*, 2(31), 24–37.

ENDNOTES

[1]   Where the owner is the shareholder with the majority of invoices.

[2]   http://integratedreporting.org/wp-content/uploads/2011/03/IIRC-Terms-of-Reference-July-2010.pdf.

[3]   We included in the category of *managers* the economic directors, finance managers, senior associates, accounting and tax managers, senior auditors, and accounting managers. We consider that CFOs are a different category – of top management - and should be treated as so.

Chapter 3
Conceptual Model

ABSTRACT

The current chapter explains the conceptual model outlined in this manuscript: how we arrived to our original Integrated Reporting <IR> Prototype Framework. Finally, we seek to demonstrate that the information from the framework is mostly disclosed in corporate annual reports, and that there is interest for integrated reporting adoption. The IR elements from our prototype framework resulted from accountancy profession expertise (ICAEW, IFAC, FEE, and others) International Integrated Reporting Committee (IIRC) Guidelines, IFRS-IASB standards with impact on both financial and non-financial information, social audit standards (SA8000 and AA1000), or disclosure requirements set up by a Directive of the European Union.

INTRODUCTION

During the next paragraphs, we shall explain each research area and the distribution of the 43 questions from our questionnaire. However, we should mention first that the number of the questions is the ones from the questionnaire and the way in which they are grouped in areas of interest does not correspond to the order they appear in the questionnaire (Appendix 5). This order was applied based on the fact that it would provide a plus of comprehensiveness from the respondent's side.

DOI: 10.4018/978-1-5225-2753-4.ch003

IIRC itself proposed for consultation their Framework perspective on the interaction with other reports: "The IR process is intended to be applied continuously to all relevant reports and communications, in addition to the preparation of an integrated report. The integrated report may include links to other reports and communications, e.g., financial statements and sustainability reports" (IIRC, 2013a, p. 2). We extended this vision on IR by formulating seven questions that fall under the category of interaction between financial and non-financial information; IR versus other reports:

Q2: Do you believe that nowadays it is enough for a company to comply with requirements on financial information?

This particular question is based on GRI comments made to the IIRC draft consultation framework that mention that financial information is not sufficient for conveying all the relevant information needed in decision-making processes (especially for investors).

Q5: Do you consider that current Annual Financial Reports issued by global corporations are too long, too complex, and ambiguous?
Q6: Can IR reduce complexity and ambiguity in reporting?

The formulation of the above inquiries (Q5 and Q6) comes from Farrar (2011) assumption that complexity and extended reports should be avoided and integrated reports used instead.

Q7: Are standalone IR reports the only way of practicing integrated reporting?

According to IFAC, IR practice can mean both having a standalone integrated report, or transforming previous reports (e.g., the annual report) into an integrated one (from the comment letter sent by IFAC to the IIRC Consultation Framework). The same approach is taken by ICAEW, with the specification to have interactions between the integrated report and the other reports (comment letter to the IIRC Consultation Framework).

The next three questions (Q8, Q9, and Q10) are introduced by the ACCA comments for the IIRC Consultation Framework: "IR initiative offers a significant opportunity for the quality of corporate reporting to be improved by giving to investors and others a more complete view of the entity and its prospects over a longer time frame than is usually covered in traditional corporate reporting." FEE goes further stipulating the idea of 'transition' to integrated reporting (Q8), with "significant impact on the current corporate reporting cycle" (Q9 and Q10) (FEE comment letter to IIRC).

Q8: Do you agree that the traditional report can be a predecessor for IR adoption? (By traditional report we understand the financial oriented annual report).

Q9: Is IR the answer to the current global economic challenges?

Q10: Is IR changing corporate behavior?

The next category involves the 6 capitals and the value creation process. IIRC (2013a) stipulates that the 6 capitals should be reported on a comply or explain basis (as in case one of the capitals is not mentioned the report has to explain why is not material for the company). IFAC comments on a certain "imbalance" in case of the capitals: "allocation of all capitals can be material to key stakeholders (depending on the type and size of organization" (from comment letters). ICAEW sustains this idea, while mentioning the correlation between the financial capital and the others. Further on, integrated reporting has to contribute to the "organization's ability to create value over time" (FEE comment letter). Therefore, we have formulated the following questions:

Q33: In your opinion, a company should disclose information about all 6 of its CAPITALS (financial, human, intellectual, social, relational, natural)?

Q34: Could you please rank the capitals according to their importance (from 1->6)?

Q35: What implications can the financial capital have on the other capitals?

Q24: The IIRC mentions the importance of value creation and preservation: "Integrated Reports should enable providers of financial capital to gain an understanding of how an organization creates and sustains value in the short, medium and long term." What does the VALUE represent?

The next area of interest is linked to the purpose of defining integrated reporting which contains five questions:

Q21: What do you understand by INTEGRATION as a process of the IR?

It is essential to understand the integration process, from sustainability perspectives (Krajnc & Glavic, 2005), to economic, social, environmental impacts (Wilkinson *et al.*, 2004), or the interdependence/correlation between financial and non-financial information (IIRC, 2013).

Q22: Which is the difference between CONNECTIVITY and INTERCONNECTION?

IR should also be assessed starting from the interconnectivity of economic, social, and environmental disclosure (Watson and Monterio, 2011, Wilkinson et al., 2004) or the connection between companies' activities that create value (Winter, 2012).

As ICAEW and FEE insist on good practice examples for IR adoption and implementation (comment letters), we formulated other three questions:

Q23: How can companies CONNECT internal and external information?

Q23 arises at the following remarks made by Corporate Responsibility Performance Manager Lauren Owens from National Australia Bank Ltd (member of Pillot Programme): "For us the exciting new development has been making connections with different business areas. For the first time, we're trying to incorporate key corporate responsibility information in the strategic section of our Annual Review to explain links to the delivery of strategic objectives such as strengthening our Australian business and enhancing our reputation. Different parts of the business now have an on-going dialogue to achieve a mutual understanding of how information connects and what the most material extra-financial risks are, such as reputation and customer retention, or environmental impacts in lending and financing activities; integration across silos. Breaking down barriers between departments has led to stronger cross-functional communications and more integrated thinking".

Q26: Do you think that the progress so far in IR is creating connections/links between departments and people (internal stakeholders)?

Q26 is based on the example of HSBC Company from Pillot Programme that incorporates more financial oriented and less integrating non-financial data. Also, HSBC's finance function acts as a filter for data collection and processing, making it easier to identify the financial implications of environmental, social and human capital issues.

Q27: How should information be communicated in IR?

HSBC's Sustainability Report provides detailed information on its business strategy, how it serves customers, its response to climate change, sustainability risk management – such as lending guidelines, the measures it takes to meet internal environmental efficiency targets, employee and community investment programmes, along with relevant key data; connectivity between the business model, values, strategy, performance, financial information, risks, governance and regulatory information; connectivity between strategy, KPIs and performance; discipline of reporting economic, social and environmental performance is contributing to the assessment of interrelationship between elements of the business.

Another research area (IR costs and benefits) refers to the costs of issuing integrated reports (ICAEW comment letter), identifying the beneficiaries in terms of financial capitals providers or all stakeholders (IFAC comment letter), and providing examples from reporting practice related to IR benefits (ACCA comment letter), to finally manage to understand the importance of a cost- benefit analysis (from IFAC comment letter): "The practical issue, however, is whether certain information can become available at a reasonable cost/benefit level...the Framework should also enable organizations to include cost/benefit analysis in their considerations on application of the Framework". Below you can find the questions included in this category:

Q4: Why should companies report on non- financial information?

The international non-financial reporting initiatives taken by various countries (South Africa where IR is mandatory, Denmark, Norway, and Sweden that regulate sustainability reporting (Eccles et al., 2010a), and France where non-listed corporations have to report on environmental and social information according to Grenelle II legislation) would generate, in time, more non-financial reports. However, besides the legislative pressure, organizations have to understand the benefits derived from this type of reporting.

Q14: Who should be more interested in reading the integrated reports?

It is essential for prepares of annual reports to fully understand the needs of users (Slack, 2006). In addition, any integrated should have a target audience, and it should make clear whether it mainly addresses providers of financial capital (investors), or all stakeholders.

Q19: Do you agree that IR should be investor oriented?

Q19 brings into attention the investor perceived as the most important category of stakeholder. ICAEW sustains this fact as IR shows "businesses and their investors that sustainable business practices are consistent with their long-term interests" (from the comment letter).

Q20: Do you agree that the IR framework should concentrate more on shareholder value (and the regular investor) instead of setting disclosure rules for SRI (Social Responsible Investors)?

Q20 was formulated based on ICAEW assumptions made in their comment letter to the IIRC Consultation Framework: "We are concerned that illustrations and language in the draft framework may reinforce the view that <IR> is purely or mainly for SRI investors, and we would encourage the IIRC to emphasize how information provided in accordance with the framework should support fundamentals-based assessments of shareholder value".

Q25: In your opinion, which are the outcomes of an IR?

IFAC, ICAEW, and ACCA suggested that the notion of outcomes creates confusion in the IIRC Consultation Draft. Further on, it has been advised that the definition is explained more clearly: "outcomes are the impacts of outputs that are used in achieving the reporting entity's objectives" (IFAC comment letter).

Q28: Who are the users of an IR?

Although in the comment letter FEE applauds the decision of IIRC to focus on investors as primary users of IR, we consider that the other stakeholders should also be taken into account as reporting audience. Q28 is meant to express the opinion of members from accounting professional bodies on the IR users.

Q29: Can IR bring 'rewards' for internal and external stakeholders?

In IFAC's vision' rewards are incorporated into value for stakeholders: "An organization can create and maximize value by serving the interests of, and working with, all its key stakeholders" (Comment letter).

Q30: Who are the beneficiaries of IR?

FEE's perspective that all stakeholders should benefit from IR is debatable as the same accounting profession body agrees on maintaining investors as top priority before the other stakeholders.

Q31: What are the benefits of IR?

As mentioned before, IR can provide the socially responsible investor and analyst (Radley, 2012) all the necessary information for making decisions. Other benefits include community and social programmes (Henderson et al., 1980; Deegan and Rankin, 1996), improving sustainability practices at national levels, reporting transparency, stakeholder engagement, (ACCA, 2012), improvements in resource allocation, reputation (Eccles and Saltzman, 2011).

Q32: What are the limitations of IR?

The main limitations for IR were underlined by Loska (2011) as effective communication; connection between financial and non-financial information; establishing the IFRS perspective upon integrated reporting; the definition of sustainability.

The next research area involves a discussion of IR determinants and is made of three questions:

Q11: Why do you believe organizations publish these IR?

The first question (above) is based on accounting theories (positive accounting theory, agency theory, diffusion and adoption theory, legitimacy theory, institutional theory, stakeholder theory and shareholder theory) according to which stakeholders' pressure or fulfilling stakeholders' needs, cost reduction and controlling, efficient resource allocation, eliminate information asymmetry, contribute to the issuance of integrated reports.

Q12: Do you think companies are self- motivated to publish these reports or they do it for marketing/image purposes (other reasons – please mention them)?

We formulated Q12 in correlation to literature evidence: Farrar (2011) argues that sustainability reporting is driven by reputational insights and can be seen as a marketing strategy. In addition, a survey conducted by ACCA claims the need for IR that would convey a better image for the company itself (ACCA, 2014). Finally, Eccles and Saltzman (2011) mention that reputation is one of the benefit of IR.

Q13: Which of the following external forces should influence the issuance of IR as an organization reporting behavior?

We used institutional theory to show that that the economic, cultural, social, political, and other factors maintain a significant influence upon worldwide organizations (Jackson & Apostolakou, 2010; Matten & Moon, 2008; Granovetter, 2000; Granovetter, 1985).

The recommendations concerning the IIRC Framework represents the next research area that contains 4 questions:

Q15: The IIRC framework is developed on a set of components (elements): organizational overview and business model; operating context, including risks and opportunities; strategic objectives and strategies to achieve those objectives; governance and remuneration; performance; future outlook. Which elements should be excluded from the framework and why?

Q16: What new elements should be added to the framework and why?

Q17: The IIRC framework contains also a set of principles: strategic focus; connectivity of information; future orientation; responsiveness and stakeholder inclusiveness; conciseness, reliability and materiality. Which principles should be excluded from the framework and why?

Q18: What new principles should be added to the framework and why?

These questions arisen from a need to "explain the extent to which… the content of the Framework…is appropriate for use by organizations in preparing an integrated report and for providing report users with information about an organization's ability to create value in the short, medium and long term" and from an identified need to "develop explanatory material on IR in addition to the Framework" (IIRC, 2013a, pp. 14-15).

The industry research area contains two questions:

Q36: Do you believe that all companies should be held accountable in front of society?

Q 36 is formulated based on the fact that industry segments influences reporting habits (Buniamin, 2012; Patten, 1991).

Q37: Should the IIRC framework be adapted to each sector? (e.g., banks and insurance companies are less harmful to environment than chemical companies).

The IIRC view contradicts the idea that the IR framework has to be flexible according to industry's specificity, stating that integrated reporting adoption should remove the country and industry barriers and result in a single corporate reporting norm (IIRC, 2013).

Another research theme makes reference to characteristics for IR information (Q3 and Q38).

Q3: What do you understand by relevant information?

FEE provided feedback to IIRC on relevant information disclosure mentioning that this should not be included in the category of confidential information (comment letter). Therefore, it is important that the relevance character of the information from the IR is correctly assimilated and understood.

Q38: What information should be material for an IR?

Regarding the materiality characteristic, FEE suggests that IIRC differentiates between the materiality for investors and the one for the other groups of stakeholders (comment letter).

The introduction of the last theme in our questionnaire is prevailed by the IIRC initiative to "create an online database of authoritative sources of indicators or measurement methods developed by established reporting standard setters and others" and main dilemma for whether assurance should be provided for the some parts of the report only, or for the entire report (IIRC, 2013a). This research topic contains four questions.

Q39: Integrated Reporting should be: voluntary/mandatory

ACCA' position on voluntary versus mandatory IR is the following: "We would not encourage IIRC to promote mandatory application of <IR> by jurisdictions at this stage, given the lack of track record and examples, but rather promote this as a market-led initiative. We are aware of course that in some cases such best practice initiatives do not meet … much success, and that without mandation or strong endorsement from regulators …adoption of IR will make slow progress in those places. But we believe mandatory application is not appropriate at a time when IIRC will benefit more from allowing companies to experiment and evolve good practice, and develop the overall track record of application of the framework" (from the comment letter).

Q41: Does the corporate reporting environment need a global STANDARD for IR?

ICAEW rejects the IIRC's initiative of having an online database with authoritative sources, as IIRC itself is not a professional accounting body (comment letter). Therefore, the issue of having a global standard for IR – from the initiative of IR- is questionable.

Q42: Which policy makers/professional bodies/members of professional bodies is more suitable for issuing such a standard?

IFAC proposes that GRI and the Greenhouse Gas Protocol, as well as national laws or industry requirements could be involved in the development of IR standards (comment letter). However, we consider that the list can be extended to IASB-FASB, SASB, and even IIRC (but only as an advisor or consultant and not policy makers/professional bodies/member of professional bodies).

Q40: Do you believe it is too early to consider the assurance, perhaps via some kind of independent 'audit' report, of IR?

IFAC comments on IR assurance stated the difficulty to apply assurance for certain topics from the integrated report, such as forward looking information (comment letter). Therefore, it is suggested the idea that only some parts of the report are auditable. ICAEW (comment letter) argues for patience in what regards IR assurance, while FEE (comment letter) mentions the need for audit standards issued by International Auditing and Assurance Standards Board (IAASB).

In 2013, European Commission issued an official document – Proposal for a Directive of the European Parliament and of the Council – regarding disclosure of non- financial and diversity information by certain large companies and groups. This Directive suggests the introduction of two additional reporting statements (a non-financial statement and a corporate governance statement). These should contain non- financial information (environmental/social/employee- related, anti-corruption/bribery etc.) and information on diversity (age/gender etc.). These elements comply with the IIRC vision of integrating financial, social, economic, and governance related information (IIRC, 2012). Figure 1 outlines our vision on IR, in its evolution, from voluntary to mandatory requirements, as the European Union already regulates non-financial information disclosure for its members, while IASB manifested a strong interest in setting global reporting rules for IR, in the form of future standards or norms.

Figure 1. Our vision on the evolution of integrated reporting
Source: author's design

	Europe – UE	Global		
IIRC	FEE	IFAC		IASB/FASB
Voluntary				*Mandatory*
	Discussing the framework	Focus on investors (or all stakeholders?)	Regulation (UNEP, 2009)	
		Demand/need for Social, Environmental, governance information	----------→	

Figure 2. IR elements and principles
Source: author's design

CONTENT ELEMENTS	PRINCIPLES
Mission	Strategic focus
Vision	Future orientation
Strategy	Connectivity of information
Business Model	Stakeholder responsiveness
Performance	Materiality
Governance	Conciseness
Future outlook	Reliability
Opportunities	Completeness
Risks	Consistency
Report preparation	Comparability
Report presentation	

Furthermore, according to IIRC, integrated reports should provide a list of elements and principles that have been also considered in our developed research framework prototype (Figure 2).

Research modeling assumes the usage of certain variables. It is important to distinguish between the types of variables. These are the main categories of research variables: independent variable, explanatory variable, dependent variable, moderating variable (or dichotomous variable), intervening variable, and extraneous variable (Figure 3).

Figure 3 contains the elements extracted from accounting standards and used in our framework disclosure index on integrated reporting. The section

Figure 3. Research variables and the connection between them
Source: adapted after Smith (2003)

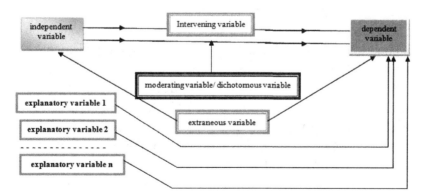

on environmental information was adapted after a study developed by Barbu et al. (2012), while the CSR information is partially contained within IAS 37: recognition of provision (CPA, 2013), and IFRS 8: disclosure on CSR information (EC, 2013). IFRS 6 standard on Exploration for and Evaluation of Mineral Resources contains reporting guidelines on extractive activities, providing details on the recognition of mineral resources as assets and other environmental expenses: "Exploration and evaluation assets will be treated as a separate class of assets for disclosure purposes" (extracted from IFRS 6). Therefore, the following two disclosure items from IFRS 6 were considered in our framework, namely: intangible assets exploration of mineral resources and other environmental expenses. IAS 36 Impairment of Assets refers, among others, to the environmental assets of an entity that are subject to impairment, because of accident, depletion or contamination of mineral resources, loosing contractual rights etc. According to the standard, the impairment applies to intangible and tangible assets (including those related to the exploration of mineral resources). Thus, we considered the next disclosure items to be part of our IR conceptual framework: intangible and tangible assets exploration of mineral resources, intangible assets that do not involve mineral resources (emission rights assets[1]; concessions, licenses, trademarks, and similar items; other intangible assets), and tangible assets not related to mineral resources. The tangible assets concerning mineral resources exploration are also contained in IFRIC 6 interpretation: Liabilities Arising from Participating in a Specific Market – Waste Electrical and Electronic Equipment that assume the recognition of a liability on waste management cost regarding electronic equipment. IAS 38 standard on Intangible Assets include information on how the environmental assets should be measured and recognized. According to the accounting referential, the recognition takes place if "it is probable that the expected future economic benefits that are attributable to the asset will flow to the entity; and the cost of the asset can be measured reliably" (extracted from IAS 38). The measurement has to be done at cost model or revaluation model: An entity shall choose either the cost model or the revaluation model as its accounting policy (extracted from IAS 38). The impairment has to be applied for the following intangible assets from our framework: emission rights assets; concessions, licenses, trademarks, and similar items; other intangible assets; other environmental expenses). IAS 16 Property, plant and equipment indicates is related to the purchase tangible (fixed) assets, their recognition, carrying amount determination, and depreciation. The recognition of the asset should take place if: "it is probable that future economic benefits associated with the item will flow to the entity; and the cost of the item can be measured reliably" (extracted from IAS 16). If interpret this the other way around, it results that 'future economic benefits may be compromised in the absence of certain environmental assets, even though the latter are only accessories to the main operation' (Barbu et al., 2012, p. 17). In addition, IAS 16 mentions that the cost of property, plant and equipment has to include 'the initial estimate of the costs of dismantling and removing the item and restoring the site on which it is located' (extracted from IAS 16). According to Barbu et al. (2012, p. 17) 'these costs are estimated at the beginning of the asset's useful life, and are assimilated to a provision in compliance with IAS 37. Future expenses with dismantling and site restoration may also be derived as a consequence of the continuous use of an asset whose environmental impact is not negligible'. IAS 2 on Inventories is applied in case of companies with a high pollution degree, for example from mining industry. According to the standard, waste has to be recognized as assets at a residual value. On the other hand, when converted into a tradable good, and additional costs are applied, the waste should be recognized under the form of inventories. IAS 20 Accounting for Government Grants explains among others how emission rights are distributed and how should they be recognized in financial statements. IAS 37 Provisions, Contingent Liabilities and Contingent Assets mention the recognition and measurement of provisions, contingent liabilities and contingent assets. A provision represents a liability that should be recognized if: "an entity has a present obligation (legal or constructive) as a result of) a past event; it is probable that an outflow of resources embodying economic benefits will be required to settle the obligation an outflow of future economic benefits is to be expected in this circumstance; a reliable estimate can be made of the amount of the obligation" (extracted from the standard). The contingent liability represents "a possible obligation that arises from past events and whose existence will be confirmed only by the occurrence or non-occurrence of one or more uncertain future events not wholly within the control of the entity; or (b) a present obligation that arises from past events but is not recognized (extracted from the standard). The contingent asset "arises from past events and whose existence will be confirmed only by the occurrence or non-occurrence of one or more uncertain future events not wholly within the control of the entity" (extracted from the standard). IAS 8 Accounting policies, changes in accounting estimates and errors do not refer directly to environmental expenses. However, the standard mentions that its guidelines can be implemented for companies that modify the estimation of environmental provisions or make

Table 1. Elements from IFRS/IASB standards included in our framework on IR

Environmental Information				
Intangible assets exploration of mineral resources	IFRS 6	IAS 36		
Emission rights assets	IAS 38	IAS 36	IFRIC 3	
Concessions, licenses, trademarks, and similar items	IAS 38	IAS 36		
Other intangible assets	IAS 38	IAS 36		
Tangible assets	IAS 16	IAS 36		
Tangible assets with exploration of minerals resources	IFRIC 6	IAS 36		
Inventories (waste)	IAS 2			
Environmental provisions (provision for dismantling, removal of assets and the site restoration, Provision for CO2 emissions, Provision for insurance, environmental litigates etc.)	IAS 37	IFRIC 5	IFRIC 6	IFRIC 1	IFRIC 3
Emission rights governmental grant	IAS 20	IFRIC 3		
Fines and taxes for environmental purposes	IAS 37			
Other environmental expenses	IAS 8	IAS 38	IFRS 6	
Contingent liabilities and assets	IAS 37			
CSR Information				
Recognition of Provision	IAS 37			
present obligation				
outflow of resources				
reasonable estimate				
Disclosure on CSR Information	IFRS 8			
commitment to transparency				
acceptance on obligation to societies in which they work				
avoid reputation risk				
commitment to investors				
CSR information included in financial statements				
CSR information subject to statutory audit				

Source: adapted after Barbu et al. (2012), EC (2013), and CPA (2013)

adjustments/ corrections on environmental costs. IFRS 8 Operating segments make reference to "environmental services and environmental protection, such as clean energy, urban services, decontamination services, and recycling, green technologies" (Brabu et al., 2012, p. 19).

The final stage of our model consists of the two dimensions of the social audit: SA 8000 and AA 1000 standards requirements. SA 8000 standard includes elements of child labor, forced and compulsory labor, health and safety, freedom of association and right to collective bargaining, discrimination, disciplinary practices, working hours, remuneration, and management systems. AA 1000 states the three principles of inclusivity, materiality, and responsiveness. In our view, social audit represent the first step in auditing integrated reports, focusing on the non- financial elements and how these are influenced by the financial area.

The Figure 5 describes our conceptual framework/ model on integrated reporting. Our purpose is to investigate whether companies disclose these elements in their annual reports. In order to check the mentioned items we used the *Tropes* software for searching the disclosure items within the companies' annual reports. This software performs semantic content analysis on texts and was included in various research studies for measuring the level of information impact (Vander Putten and Nolen, 2010), and helps to identify how different types of disclosure (financial/non-financial-CSR-sustainability)

Figure 4. Social audit requirements
Source: author's design

Social audit	
SA 8000	**AA 1000**
Child labor	Inclusivity
Forced labor	Materiality
Compulsory labor	Responsiveness
Health and Safety	Integrate with governance
Freedom of Association	Integrate with organizational strategy and operations management
Right to Collective Bargaining	Purpose of stakeholder engagement
Discrimination	Stakeholder identification
Disciplinary Practices	Profile and map stakeholders
Working Hours	Determine engagement level and method
Remuneration	
Management Systems	

Figure 5. From accounting theories to regression models
Source: author's design

can contribute to a better communication between the preparers and users of corporate reports (Mohamed & Daniel, 2012).

Three of the variables from our model - year, country, and industry - belong to both institutional theory and PAT, as external factors from certain time intervals, such as post-crises periods, inflation, or other economic circumstances that took place in one year or another, have an influence upon organizational behavior and corporate reporting, in the same time predicting the trend in disclosure. The same applies for different industry segments that can exert pressure in the respective sectors, as well as the country variable, corresponding to national legal enforcements.

1. **Year, Country, Industry, Accounting Standard:** Some of the most common used variables for measuring the effect against disclosure levels in corporations' reports are time period/year, country, industry, and accounting policies/standards (Hackston & Milne, 1996; Marston, 2003; Alford et al., 1993; Rob & Zarzeski, 2001; Hope, 2003). In an attempt to find associations between financial and non- financial disclosure versus profitability, scholars and academics choose different time intervals in their analysis and regressions- from one year (Botosan, 1997; Botosan, 2002; Sengupta, 1998; Mitchell et al., 1995) to an extended time frame (Hughes, 2000; Nicolaj et al., 2005; Williams, 2001). Research studies show the low impact of the countries in which corporations are operating upon the non- financial disclosures in their reports, especially for Anglo-American countries – Australia, Canada, the United States (Robb & Zarzeski, 2001), and European region (Vanstraelen et al., 2003). On the other hand, Patten (1991), argues that industry is highly correlated with disclosure on environmental and social information, and the analysis

developed by Hackston and Milne (1996) prove that same results apply for New Zealand case.

2. **Company Size:** The company size, measured by its total assets (TA) and number of employees, has always been correlated with financial and non-financial disclosures in previous research studies (Thomas, 1986; Morhardt, 2010; Aras et al., 2010). Some academics and scholars have found that the company size registers significant correlations with social and environmental disclosures (Hackston & Milne, 1986). Further on, international literature contains various debates on the influence of company size on the CSR behavior, firm performance, and stakeholder engagement, as large firms are more stakeholders oriented, have higher performance, and adopt faster CSR policies (Ullman, 1985; Burke et al., 1986). Other researchers consider that there is high connection between the disclosure of information and the companies' size (Craven & Marston, 2010). Wallace and Nasser (1995) discuss the implications of total assets and sales (as size variables) on disclosures in annual reports. Hackston and Milne (1996) and Patten (1991) admit that company size is positively correlated with the disclosure on social and environmental information. Therefore, we consider that the company size is an important indicator for explaining the disclosure in integrated reports.

3. **Price per Share, Market Value, Operating Income, Debt to Equity:** Academics and scholars have often associated market value and price per share with the corporate voluntary disclosure (Eng & Mark, 2003; Healy & Palepu, 2001; McNally et al., 1982). In addition, operating income is another factor that influences corporate disclosure (Botosan, 2000; Mitchell et al., 1995), along with debt to equity ratio (Malone et al., 1993; Lopes & de Alencar, 2010). Through analogy, all these variables should contribute to the publication of integrated reports.

4. **Market Capitalization:** Hackston and Milne (1996) underline the importance of introducing market capitalization as a factor for measuring disclosures in companies' reports. Jaggi and Low (2000) study the impact of market capitalization on disclosure of financial information. However, when it comes to non-financial information disclosure and its association with capital markets, there is not so many evidence in international literature. The connection between market capitalization and environmental information focused on pollution issues (Gupta & Goldar, 2006), environmental performance (Palmer et al., 1995; Porter & Van der Linde, 1995), and measures of performance (Al-Tuwaijri et al., 2004; Konar & Kohen, 2001). Another element that links the non-financial

information with the capital markets is the socially responsible investor (Radley, 2012) who rely on this type of information in the decision-making process (Berthelot et al., 2003; Richardson & Welker, 2001). Studies on voluntary disclosure show that the volume of information provided by corporate reports is strongly influenced by the needs of investors, stakeholder engagement, and market capitalization (Boesso & Kumar, 2007). Since we mentioned the importance of market capitalization for financial and non-financial information disclosure, there is no doubt that integrated reports (as a mixture of financial and non-financial data) will be determined, among others, by capital markets.

5. **Gross Domestic Product (GDP):** Research on corporate disclosure reveals that companies operating in developing countries are more eager to present information on a voluntary basis (Islam & Deegan, 2008), especially of non-financial nature (Neumayer & Perkins, 2004). In addition, various researchers have associated the GBP – Gross Domestic Product, with corporate disclosure (Jaggi & Low, 2000; Ballou et al., 2013). We should also mention the paper developed by Jensen and Berg (2011) that proves the connection between integrated reports and countries' GDP.

6. **Legal Origin (Civil Law Country/Common Law Country):** Empirical research (Jensen & Berg, 2011) divides the political factor of institutionalism between common law- in which shareholder primacy applies- and civil law political systems- where reporting transparency, non-financial information stakeholder theory are promoted. In a much broader context, Friedman's theory claim for shareholders' ownership, while Freeman agrees upon the fact that all the stakeholders should exert the control over the company in an equally manner (Stars & Bainbridge, 2013). According to Aceituno et al. (2012) the political factor has impact on integrated reports, the diffusion and adoption of IR being representative for civil law countries.

7. **Human Development Index (HDI):** The Human Development Index (UNDP, 2013), have a strong social construct and a special ability to provide an accurate classification, by its social attributes. Also, we expected to find a higher score on IR disclosure for the companies from lower developed countries given the fact that these countries have greater social problems and may disclose more information regarding the proposed solutions and outcomes in connection to these problems.

8. **Corruption Perception Index (CPI):** Ranking the corruption degree for a country's public sector, Corruption Perception Index- CPI data

is provided for no less than 175 countries and regions (Transparency International, 2013). Moreover, CSR disclosure has often been measured against CPI- Corruption Perception Index (Baughn & McIntosh, 2007; Hilson, 2012; Wiig & Ramalho, 2005), and sustainability information can be correlated to the level of the same CPI (Schadewitz & Niskala, 2010; Haufler, 2010). In previous sections of the thesis, we have managed to demonstrate that CSR and sustainability information are elements of the integrated report. Therefore, we can deduct that IR will be influenced by the CPI.

REFERENCES

Barbu, E., Dumontier, P., Feleaga, N., & Feleaga, L. (2012). *Mandatory environmental disclosures by companies complying with IAS/IFRS: The case of France, Germany and the UK*. Retrieved from http://halshs.archives-ouvertes.fr/docs/00/65/87/34/PDF/CR_2011-09_E2.pdf

CPA. (2013). *Viewpoint: Applying IFRS IFRSs in the Mining Industry, Recognition of Corporate Social Responsibility Provision under IAS 37*. Retrieved from http://www.cica.ca/applying-the-standards/financial-reporting/international-financial-reporting-standards/item75115.pdf

European Commission. (2013). *Proposal for a Directive of the European Parliament and of the Council*. Available online at http://ec.europa.eu/dgs/home-affairs/e-library/documents/categories/proposed-legislation/index_en.htm

Smith, M. (2003). *Research Methods in Accounting*. London: SAGE Publication. doi:10.4135/9781849209809

Vander Putten, J., & Nolen, A. L. (2010). Comparing results from constant comparative and computer software methods: A reflection about qualitative data analysis. *Journal of Ethnographic and Qualitative Research, 5*, 99–112.

ENDNOTE

[1]   IFRIC 3 Interpretation explains that rights/ allowances represent intangible assets and have to be included in financial statements as IAS 38 Intangible Assets specifies. Therefore, emission rights are considered as a category of intangible assets. Although withdraw in 2005, IFRIC 3 remains the only interpretation on emission rights accounting treatment, as there has not been issued any other in replacement.

Chapter 4
Discussion of Results

ABSTRACT

This chapter presents and discusses the results of our analysis. Regarding the findings our first research study, the questionnaire on IR, we organize the discussion of results into more sections, namely research area (1) the interaction between the financial and non-financial information; IR versus other reports; research area (2) the capitals and the value creation process; research area (3) defining integrated reporting; research area (4) IR costs and benefits; research area (5) determinants of integrated reporting; research area (6) recommendations concerning the IIRC framework; research area (7) the industry; research area (8) characteristics for IR information; research area (9) voluntary versus mandatory IR and assurance. The second part of our research presents the results of the SPSS analysis, and we interpret the data according to its economic and business significance.

INTRODUCTION

We begin by outlining the results obtained in our first research study: the questionnaire on IR content and adoption, addressed to accountancy profession.

The questionnaire had an average response rate of 22%. This percentage represents the average of the answers received per question from the total number of respondents: 69 (100%). We are going to analyze the answers and present the main arguments of the respondents, where the case.

DOI: 10.4018/978-1-5225-2753-4.ch004

Research Area 1: The Interaction Between the Financial and Non-Financial Information - IR vs. Other Reports

If we analyze the trends in the replies received from the members of accounting professional bodies in what regards research area (1) the interaction between financial and non-financial information and between corporate reports (Chart no. 1), shows that according to most of the respondents in Q10 (13 people) IR is changing corporate behavior, as investors need non-financial information for decision-making purposes (Q2 – feedback from 51 people). IR represents the global solution for worldwide economic challenges (Q9 with a maximum of 21 respondents), and acts like a catalyzer generating a shift in corporate reporting, from the traditional report to the integrated report (not necessarily a separate report): 29 people answered that standalone IR reports are not the only way of practicing IR (Q7), while 37 consider that traditional reports contain elements of an IR (Q8). Also, the results suggest that the complexity, ambiguity, and length of the annual reports can be reduced only in case of large companies (Q5 and Q6).

Further on, we are going to analyses in more detail the answers provided in each of the question included in research area 1.

74% of the interviewed practitioners and professional accountants consider that compliance with financial information requirements is not enough for a corporation, because nowadays investors rely on non- financial information also when making decisions. Only 5 responders did not agree that the non-

Figure 1. The trend in responses received for research area 1
(Source: author's design)

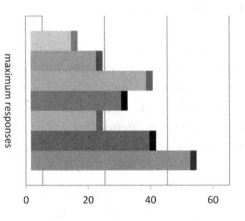

IR is changing corporate behavior, educating corporations to become more socially responsible in front of society
IR is the answer to the current global economic challenges

traditional reports contain elements of an IR

standalone IR reports are not the only way of practicing IR

IR can reduce complexity in annual reports for large companies only

Annual Financial Reports issued by global corporations are too long, too complex, and ambiguous are not too long and complex

financial information is as important as the financial one when making decisions or serving investments analysis models. This particular question had a very good response rate of 81% (a small number of 13 people out of 69 chosen not to reply).

Surprisingly, more than half of our respondents consider that annual financial reports are not too long, complex, and ambiguous. We would have expected a higher rate for an opposite answer, as the integrated reporting idea is based on the statement that annual financial reports issued by corporations are long, complex, and ambiguous, so that the users of these reports find it difficult to understand them: "All matters which are important in assessing an organization's performance and position, past and prospective, need to be reported but not by making annual reports ever longer and more complex – they are too long already. The information needs to be provided clearly and concisely with the connections between financial, environmental and social impacts demonstrated and the clutter removed. This is what Integrated Reporting seeks to achieve (Sir Michael Peat, Chairman of the IIRC). "Only 4 people agree that annual financial reports are long, complex, and ambiguous. They motivate their choice with specific examples: "Form 30 from the Romanian regulation on annual financial statements contains allot of redundant information, because most of it is included in detail in the explanatory notes, or there are distinct statements (other than annual financial statements) in which they are reported (e.g. information related to interests, dividends, royalties, grants, etc.)"; "All non-performance information (financial and fiscal) is useless to a non-financial expert because no conclusions can be made. A potential investor can understand basic KPIs, simplified results and

Table 1.

No.	Question	Type of Q	Response Rate
Q2.	Do you believe that nowadays it is enough for a company to comply with requirements on financial information?	CLOSED	81%
(no answer)		13	19%
A1	no, because nowadays investors rely on non- financial information also (besides the financial one) when making decisions	51	74%
A2	yes, non-financial information is not important in decision- making processes	1	1%
A3	yes, only financial information is relevant for investors	4	6%
TOTAL RESPONDENTS		69	100%

basic financial notes. Certain type of extra information (e.g. how is the cost of sales calculated or the distribution and other costs in the profit and loss; what items form the cash flow; what are the changes in equity) will be truly understood only if the user/ potential investor studied financial accounting". In addition, those who provided an affirmative answer mentioned explicitly that in their opinion information related to business review, interests, dividends, royalties, grants should be excluded from the annual report: In this case we have a response rate of 61%.

However, a significant percentage (30%) of the respondents believes that IR can reduce complexity and ambiguity in reporting for large companies only, while 17% include the Small and Medium Enterprises also. Only 7 out of 69 participants do not agree that IR contributes to a decrease in reporting's complexity and ambiguity. The respondents' rate overcomes 50%.

Table 2.

No.	Question	Type Of Q	Response Rate
Q5.	Do you consider that current Annual Financial Reports issued by global corporations are too long, too complex, and ambiguous?	CLOSED	61%
(no answer)		27	39%
A1	Yes	4	6%
A2	No	38	55%
TOTAL RESPONDENTS		69	100%

Table 3.

No.	Question	Type Of Q	Response Rate
Q6.	Can IR reduce complexity and ambiguity in reporting?	CLOSED	58%
(no answer)		29	42%
A1	yes, in some cases - for large companies only, but not for Small Medium Enterprises	21	30%
A2	yes, in all cases;	12	17%
A3	No	7	10%
TOTAL RESPONDENTS		69	100%

According to 42% of the accounting profession members, standalone IR reports are not the only way of practicing integrated reporting, as corporations can disclose integrated financial and non- financial information in a Corporate Social Responsibility/Environmental/Sustainability Report. This question had the purpose of identifying the perspective on common practices of integrated reporting. In theory, we can have both cases (the single report, or the multi-reports variants), but we needed the opinion of practitioners regarding which is the most feasible solution to be applied in practice for reducing reporting costs and enhancing more benefits. Only 14% define IR as one single report – the Annual Report - that comprises financial and non- financial informed. This question has a response rate of 57%.

54% of the practitioners agree that traditional reports contain elements of an integrated report. A small percentage (4%) believes that IR is the opposite of a traditional report. This question has a response rate of over 50%.

Table 4.

No.	Question	Type Of Q	Response Rate
Q7.	Are standalone IR reports the only way of practicing integrated reporting?	CLOSED	57%
(no answer)		30	43%
A1	yes, because IR means one single report – the Annual Report - that comprises both financial and non- financial informed	10	14%
A2	no, as corporations can disclose integrated financial and non- financial information in a Corporate Social Responsibility /Environmental / Sustainability Report	29	42%
TOTAL RESPONDENTS		69	100%

Table 4.

No.	Question	Type Of Q	Response Rate
Q8.	Do you agree that the traditional report can be a predecessor for IR adoption? (By traditional report we understand the financial oriented annual report).	CLOSED	100%
(no answer)		29	42%
A1	no: the IR is the opposite of a traditional report	3	4%
A2	yes: traditional reports contain elements of an IR	37	54%
TOTAL RESPONDENTS		69	100%

30% of the accountants consider that IR is the answer to the current global economic challenges. 6% of them strongly agree with the statement, 9% neither agree nor disagree, while 4 people disagree and 1 is not sure. Respondents were requested to explain their options. Those who filled in the option with I agree motivate their choice through different remarks:

"As economic reality changes and becomes more complex, the needs of the users of reports increase. IR will be a good option to show a complete picture of the company."; "IR can offer more details about a company"; "it can help find better result";" if annual reporting is standardized globally, this will ensure a freer circulation of significant information and help develop new investment opportunities, including for countries less fortunate in economic development and with complex fiscal systems"; "It might bring beneficial disclosures, but in the same additional burden on organizations"; "definitions and things included must be very clear in order to report correctly and not allow window-dressing"; Obviously IR cannot be the answer to all the current global economic challenges which are very complex. It can be argued, though, that such reporting will be better understood by users". The people who did not agree with the initial statement also explained their option: "I think there are other factors influencing the global economy like policy, corruption, people behavior to change and an integrated report will work only in a perfect market which is not the case at least in Eastern Europe"; "It might be a factor towards improvement but for sure not the answer... IR alone will not solve the current global economic challenges". Those who neither agrees or disagrees consider that "first we need to see how IR will be implemented inside of companies and after that to appreciate if it's enough to meet the challenges." One of the people who strongly agreed our statement adds that "In a competitive environment, more transparency is the best solution. An organization can develop to its full capacity in a society that accepts it and trusts it..."

The question registers a 52% degree of responses.

Further on, around 39% of the respondents consider that IR is changing corporate behavior by making companies aware of their impact on people, planet, and profit or by educating corporations to become more socially responsible in front of society. Only 13% believe that firms will try to use IR for marketing purposes, disclosing only the positive side of their business. More than 50% answered to this question.

Table 5.

No	Question	Type Of Q	Response Rate
Q9.	IR is the answer to the current global economic challenges.	CLOSED	52%
(no answer)		33	48%
A1	I strongly agree	4	6%
A2	I agree	21	30%
A3	I neither agree nor disagree	6	9%
A4	I disagree	4	6%
A5	I am not sure	1	1%
TOTAL RESPONDENTS		69	100%

Table 6.

No.	Question	Type Of Q	Response Rate
Q10.	IR is changing corporate behavior.	CLOSED	52%
(no answer)		33	48%
A1	yes, by educating corporations to become more socially responsible in front of society	13	19%
A2	yes, by making companies aware of their impact on people, planet, and profit	14	20%
A3	no, firms will try to use IR for marketing purposes, disclosing only the positive side of their business	9	13%
TOTAL RESPONDENTS		69	100%

Research Area (2) the Capitals and the Value Creation Process

Figure 2 explains the accountancy professions' perception on value creation and 6 capitals (research area 2). The highest response rate from three questions under this category was registered for the question on reporting the 6 capitals (Q49). 20 people out of 69 consider that a company should disclose information about all 6 of its capitals. The degree in response decreases as we analyses the other two questions: on value creation (Q35) and the connection between financial capital and the other capitals (Q57). Therefore, 15 respondents agreed that value creation and preservation refers to economic and social value,

Figure 2. The trend in responses received for research area 2
(Source: author's design)

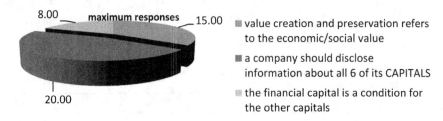

For a more accurate representation see the electronic version.

while only 8 members of accountancy profession see the financial capital as a condition for the other capitals. We made a separate chart for Q34 (Chart 3) that shows how respondents allocated the score from 1 to 6 to the capitals. The higher importance was attributed to the financial capital, on the second place was the human capital, the intellectual capital became the third, then the social capital, the relationship capital, and the last one was natural capital (14 people considered this type of capital as the last important).

Next, we are going to present the four questions related to capitals and value creation that are connected one with the other. In the first stage, we aimed to find what people believe related to the inclusion of these capitals in an annual report: should companies disclose information about all the six capitals? 29% of the professional accountants believe that a company should

Figure 3. The importance attributed to the six capitals - area 2
(Source: author's design)

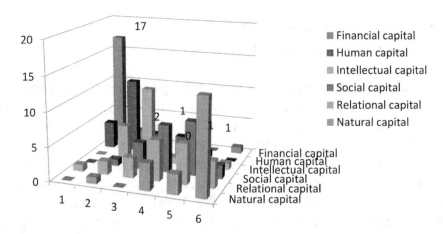

For a more accurate representation see the electronic version.

disclose information about all 6 of its capitals (financial, human, intellectual, and social, relational, natural). The ones who do not agree this statement consider that this type of information

...should remain private as it can be misleading in calculation/interpreting and the cost to provide this indicator can be higher than its usefulness to an external partner. Also due to competitive markets, you don't share everything you possess...

47 people out of 69 did not response in this case.

Secondly, we asked participants to rank the capitals from 1 to 6. Most of them indicated financial capital as being on the first place, then human capital,

Table 7.

No.	Question	Type Of Q	Response Rate
Q33.	In your opinion, a company should disclose information about all 6 of its CAPITALS (financial, human, intellectual, social, relational, natural)?	CLOSED	32%
(no answer)		47	68%
A1	Yes	20	29%
A2	No	2	3%
TOTAL RESPONDENTS		69	100%

Table 8.

Q34.	Could You Please Rank the Capitals According to Their Importance (From 1->6)?						
No.	Question	Financial Capital	Human Capital	Intellectual Capital	Social Capital	Relational Capital	Natural Capital
(no answer)		47	47	47	47	47	47
A1	1	17	4	0	0	1	0
A2	2	2	11	5	1	2	1
A3	3	1	3	11	4	3	0
A4	4	1	3	1	7	6	4
A5	5	0	1	4	8	6	3
A6	6	1	0	1	2	4	14
TOTAL RESPONDENTS		69	69	69	69	69	69

intellectual capital, social capital, relational capital, and natural capital. 32% answered to this question.

However, the result of having financial capital as first in line is contradicted by the following question, where 8 people mentioned that this form of capital is a condition for the other capitals, and only 2 believe is the most important of all capitals, while we registered one opinion that without it the business can hardly operate on the long term. Here the response rate is lower (16%).

The process of value creation and preservation was defined by 22% of the respondents as the coordinates of economic and social value, while only 7 people included the KPIs and financial performance in their definition. The response rate was 32%.

Research Area (3) Defining Integrated Reporting

The next set of questions is included in theme 3: defining integrated reporting (Chart 4). 22% of the respondents define integration as the process of integrating

Table 9.

No.	Question	Type	Response Rate
Q35	What implications can the financial capital have on the other capitals?	OPEN	16%
(no answer)		58	84%
A1	is a condition for the other capitals	8	12%
A2	is the most important of all capitals	2	3%
A3	without it the business can hardly operate on the long term	1	1%
TOTAL RESPONDENTS		69	100%

Table 10.

No.	Question	Type	Response Rate
Q24	The IIRC mentions the importance of value creation and preservation: "Integrated Reports should enable providers of financial capital to gain an understanding of how an organization creates and sustains value in the short, medium and long term." What does the VALUE represent?	CLOSED	32%
(no answer)		47	68%
A1	economic/social value	15	22%
A2	KPI's/ financial performance	7	10%
TOTAL RESPONDENTS		69	100%

Figure 4. The trend in responses received for research area 3
(Source: author's design)

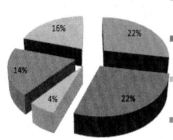

■ integration means integrating information about the business model, the 6 capitals and corporate governance

■ connectivity means creating links between the business model, values, strategy, performance, financial information, risks, governance and regulatory information, while the interconnection sets up inter-relationships between elements of the business

▩ companies connect internal and external information through analysies

■ agree that the progress so far in IR is creating connections/links between departments and people

▩ certain information should remain confidential because of competitors

*For a more accurate representation see the electronic version.

information about the business model, the 6 capitals and corporate governance. The same percentage believe connectivity means creating links between the business model, values, strategy, performance, financial information, risks, governance and regulatory information, while the interconnection sets up inter-relationships between elements of the business. 4% agree that companies connect internal and external information through analysis, 14% state that the progress so far in IR is creating connections/links between departments and people, while 16% sustain that certain information should remain confidential because of competitors.

The next stage of the analysis provides full details on the answers received per each question.

22% of the professional accountants define integration as the process of integrating information about the business model, the 6 capitals (financial, human, intellectual, social, relational, natural) and corporate governance. 7 people consider that integration means combining the Sustainability Report with the Annual Report, while 2 connected it with the integration between departments and cross-functional communications, and only one selected integrated thinking. However, the response rate is under 40%.

The next question requested participants to explain the difference between connectivity and interconnection. 22% consider that connectivity means creating links between the business model, values, strategy, performance, financial information, risks, governance and regulatory information, while the interconnection sets up inter-relationships between elements of the business. 14% mentioned that firms create connectivity between strategy, KPIs and

Table 11.

No.	Question	Type	Response Rate
Q21.	What do you understand by INTEGRATION as a process of the IR?	CLOSED	36%
(no answer)		44	64%
A1	combining the Sustainability Report with the Annual Report	7	10%
A2	integrated thinking	1	1%
A3	integrating information about the business model, the 6 capitals (financial, human, intellectual, social, relational, natural) and corporate governance	15	22%
A4	integration between departments and cross-functional communications	2	3%
TOTAL RESPONDENTS		69	100%

Table 12.

No.	Question	Type	Response Rate
Q22.	Which is the difference between CONNECTIVITY and INTERCONNECTION?	CLOSED	36%
(no answer)		44	64%
A1	connectivity means creating links between the business model, values, strategy, performance, financial information, risks, governance and regulatory information, while the interconnection sets up inter-relationships between elements of the business	15	22%
A2	firms create connectivity between strategy, KPIs and performance, and interconnection between elements of the same system/subsystem.	10	14%
TOTAL RESPONDENTS		69	100%

performance, and interconnection between elements of the same system/ subsystem. This question has the same response rate as the previous.

Only 3% of the Romanian accountancy profession members consider that companies can connect internal and external information through an integrated report. Other mean are internal and external analysis (4%), collaboration and communication (3%), strategy and planning, employees, performing IT systems, searching for logical links (1%). Less than 19% replied to this question.

18% of accountants agree that so far, the progress in IR is creating connections/links between departments and people (internal stakeholders). They add that "accomplishment of an IR supposes collaboration and communication between people and departments" and this creates an efficient

Table 13.

No.	Question	Type	Response Rate
Q23.	How can companies CONNECT internal and external information?	OPEN	19%
(no answer)		56	81%
A1	through analysis	3	4%
A2	by collaboration and communication	2	3%
A3	by strategy and planning	1	1%
A4	None	1	1%
A5	through an integrated report.	2	3%
A6	through its employees	1	1%
A7	using performing IT system	1	1%
A8	By looking at logical links	1	1%
A9	By providing comparisons between their performance and that of its competitors in the same industry, for example. Or presenting a relevant piece of external information and describing the impact it has on the internal aspects of the business.	1	1%
TOTAL RESPONDENTS		69	100%

exchange of information. 6 practitioners neither agree nor disagree with this statement (as "it depends on the company's organizational culture" and is not the main scope of IR), while 3 disagree because "IR reports are sometimes created by a special department that gathers data without understanding the

Table 14.

No.	Question	Type	Response Rate
Q26.	Do you think that the progress so far in IR is creating connections/links between departments and people (internal stakeholders)?	CLOSED	33%
(no answer)		46	67%
A1	I agree	10	14%
A2	I neither agree nor disagree	6	9%
A3	I strongly agree	3	4%
A4	I am not sure	1	1%
A5	I disagree	2	3%
A6	I strongly disagree	1	1%
TOTAL RESPONDENTS		69	100%

background", and the substance of the information. The respondents' rate is same as in previous question.

Asked about how IR should be communicated, 16% of the accounting specialists answered that certain information should remain confidential because of competitors, 8 accountants replied that negative aspects should also be revealed in order to have a transparent reporting scheme, and other 3 think that corporations should disclose as much information as possible to enhance reporting transparency. Only 32% provided feedback for this question.

Summary of Findings for Research Areas 1-3

Until now, we managed to find an answer to our first research question. Integration has been defined through the vision of accountancy profession as a function of various elements:

- Generates a shift in corporate reporting (from traditional reporting to an integrated reporting approach) that comes from the need of investors to access non-financial information for decision-making purposes;
- Has been developed as a response to global economic challenges and represents the solution for long, complex, and ambiguous traditional annual reports (at least in case of large companies);
- Is mainly explained through its 6 capitals and the value creation process, the financial capital becoming a condition for the other capitals;
- Represents, in essence, the process of integrating information about the business model, the 6 capitals and corporate governance;

Table 15.

No.	Question	Type	Response Rate
Q27.	How should information be communicated in IR?	CLOSED	32%
(no answer)		47	68%
A1	corporations should disclose as much information as possible to enhance reporting transparency	3	4%
A2	negative aspects should also be revealed in order to have a transparent reporting scheme.	8	12%
A3	certain information should remain confidential because of competitors	11	16%
TOTAL RESPONDENTS		69	100%

- Assumes connectivity of information (creating links between the business model, values, strategy, performance, financial information, risks, governance and regulatory information, while the interconnection sets up inter-relationships between elements of the business);
- Registers a positive trend or evolution by creating connections/links between departments and people and has the ability to retain that confidential information that would result in competitive disadvantage.

Research Area (4) IR Costs and Benefits

The 4th research area from our questionnaire involves the costs and benefits of IR. What we consider to be interesting if the contradictory opinion regarding the target audience for integrated reports. If at a certain point respondents answered that investors should be more interested in reading IR, being the only users for these reports, that IR are investor- oriented, integrated reports should bring 'rewards' for all stakeholders, as the outcome of IR is the image in front of clients and society. Still, shareholder values should be on the first place, business partners remaining the main beneficiaries of IR. According to most of the respondents, the main benefits of IR are better decisions, while the limitation of such a report is the issuing cost. In the end, it is agreed that non- financial information disclosure leads to reporting transparency.

Figure 5. The trend in responses received for research area (4)
(Source: author's design)

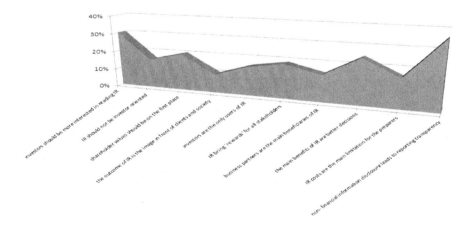

Further on, we are going to present the results obtained for each question in this category.

36% of accounting organizations members agree that corporations disclose non-financial information in their reports in order to enhance reporting transparency. 12 of the practitioners believe that the main reason for these reporting habits involve the impact on society and environment, 8 accountants think that a better image in front of stakeholders motivate companies to report on non- financial information, while 3 answered that most probably firms want to become socially responsible. This question has a very high response rate of more than 80%.

30% of the accounting profession members consider that investors should be more interested in reading those integrated reports. 7 out of the total 69 mentioned analysts as the most important category instead of investors, while 2 opted for creditors. At the other side, NGOs/ environmentalists/ other not-for-profit organizations, and governments, are the least expected to be interested in IR. The response rate is under 50%. In contrast to the opinion of accountancy profession, the IIRC perspective is that the integrated report is addressed to "all stakeholders interested in an organization's ability to create value over time, including employees, customers, suppliers, business partners, local communities, legislators, regulators and policy-makers" (IIRC, 2013, p. 7). In other words, IIRC indicates a balance between the needs and interests of all stakeholders, but still later on in the Framework, it says that the main goal of the integrated report is "explain to providers of financial capital how an organization creates value over time" (IIRC, 2013: 7), so the providers of

Table 16.

No.	Question	Type	Response Rate
Q8.	Why should companies report on non- financial information?	CLOSED	81%
(no answer)		13	19%
A1	in order to create a "better image" in front of their stakeholders	8	12%
A2	in order to become socially responsible entities	3	4%
A3	to enhance reporting transparency	25	36%
A4	because of the impact on society and environment	12	17%
A5	to gain competitive advantage	8	12%
TOTAL RESPONDENTS		69	100%

Table 17.

No.	Question	Type	Response Rate
Q14.	Who should be more interested in reading those reports?	CLOSED	46%
(no answer)		37	FALSE
A1	Creditors	2	3%
A2	Investors	21	30%
A3	Analysts	7	10%
A4	NGOs/ environmentalists/ other not-for-profit organizations	1	1%
A5	Governments	1	1%
TOTAL RESPONDENTS		69	100%

financial capital, including investors, become a privileged category of users or target audience.

16% of the answers revealed that IR should not be investor oriented as the other stakeholders have to receive equal treatment (and IR is addressed to all stakeholders- all report users are important, not only investors). 13% believe that this depends on other factors such as the size of the company and cannot be applied to SMEs, while only 9% agreed with the statement, on the motivation that investors are the main providers of financial capital. However, the response rate is only 38%.

20% of practitioners believe that in integrated reports shareholder values and the regular investor should be on the first place instead of setting disclosure rules for social responsible investors. On the other hand, 17% consider that the current reporting needs call for disclosure rules for social responsible investors. Here the response rate is also 38%.

The outcomes of an integrated report represent a deeper understanding on the needs of all stakeholders by complying with the trade-off between people, planet and profit (7%), corporations' accountability towards planet and people (3%), improved relationship with external stakeholders (4%), less pollution, efficiency in resource allocation (1%). 33% of professional accountants replied to this question.

16% of the respondents indicated that investors are the main users of an IR, while 10% mentioned internal stakeholders. By internal stakeholders they understand employees, managers, owners. The question had a 26% response rate.

Table 18.

No.	Question	Type	Response Rate
Q8.	Why should companies report on non- financial information?	CLOSED	81%
(no answer)		13	19%
A1	in order to create a "better image" in front of their stakeholders	8	12%
A2	in order to become socially responsible entities	3	4%
A3	to enhance reporting transparency	25	36%
A4	because of the impact on society and environment	12	17%
A5	to gain competitive advantage	8	12%
Q19.	Do you agree that IR should be investor oriented?	CLOSED	38%
(no answer)		43	62%
A1	no, because the other stakeholders should receive equal treatment (and IR is addressed to all stakeholders- all report users are important, not only investors).	11	16%
A2	yes, because investors are the main providers of financial capital;	6	9%
A3	this depends on other factors such as the size of the company (cannot be applied to SMEs for example)	9	13%
TOTAL RESPONDENTS		69	100%

Table 19.

No.	Question	Type	Response Rate
Q20.	Do you agree that the IR framework should concentrate more on shareholder value (and the regular investor) instead of setting disclosure rules for SRI (Social Responsible Investors)?	CLOSED	38%
(no answer)		43	62%
A1	the current reporting needs call for disclosure rules for social responsible investors	12	17%
A2	shareholder values and the regular investor should be on the first place	14	20%
TOTAL RESPONDENTS		69	100%

13 respondents consider that IR can bring 'rewards' for internal and external stakeholders.

…Integrated reporting shows a more extensive picture of essential historical financial information and more future-oriented information. By analyzing this

Discussion of Results

Table 20.

No.	Question	Type	Response Rate
Q25.	In your opinion, which are the outputs of an IR?	CLOSED	33%
(no answer)		46	67%
A1	obtaining a better corporate image in front of clients, and society as a whole	7	10%
A2	deeper understanding on the needs of all stakeholders	5	7%
A3	complying with the trade-off between people, planet and profit	5	7%
A4	corporations' accountability towards planet and people	2	3%
A5	improved relationship with external stakeholders	3	4%
A6	less pollution, efficiency in resource allocation	1	1%
TOTAL RESPONDENTS		69	100%

Table 21.

No.	Question	Type	Response Rate
Q28.	Who are the users of an IR?	CLOSED	26%
(no answer)		51	74%
A1	investors only	11	16%
A2	internal stakeholders (e.g. employees)	7	10%
A3	TOTAL RESPONDENTS	69	100%

information, an interested stakeholder will be able to understand the qualitative assessment of the risks being managed and the opportunities being explored and invest the money better…Increasing transparency and extend the degree of information provided, thereby enhancing the quality of economic decisions taken on the basis of the reporting…Stakeholders as people have a set of values and expectations that can be close to those disclosed by the company or not; if future strategy and policies are close to those values, stakeholders feel they are rewarded by the company. Stakeholder can understand better the concept of value creation in the context of the different capital elements…

There is a 29% response rate for this question.

Regarding the beneficiaries of IR, most of participants selected business partners, then local communities, and on the last place there are the legislators, regulators and policy makers. Others would mention that all these categories

53

Table 22.

No.	Question	Type	Response Rate
Q29.	Can IR bring 'rewards' for internal and external stakeholders? (Please give examples of such rewards).	CLOSED	29%
(no answer)		49	71%
A1	Yes	13	19%
A2	No	7	10%
TOTAL RESPONDENTS		69	100%

Table 23.

No.	Question	Type	Response Rate
Q30.	Who are the beneficiaries of IR?	CLOSED	23%
(no answer)		53	77%
A1	business partners	10	14%
A2	local communities	4	6%
A3	legislators, regulators and policy makers	2	3%
TOTAL RESPONDENTS		69	100%

are beneficiaries of IR and added the investors on the list of beneficiaries. 23% replied in this case.

According to most of the respondents, the main benefit of IR is the improvement in decision- making processes. Other benefits are increased efficiency of the reporting process and reduction of cost as information

Table 24.

No.	Question	Type	Response Rate
Q31,	What are the benefits of IR?	CLOSED	32%
(no answer)		47	68%
A1	improvement in decision- making processes	17	25%
A2	increased efficiency of the reporting process	4	6%
A3	reduction of cost as information is readily available, and fewer resources need to be put into research	1	1%
TOTAL RESPONDENTS		69	100%

is readily available, and fewer resources need to be put into research. 32% answered to this question.

16% of the accountants consider that the costs of preparing IR (the need for specialists; coordination of financial and non-financial information between departments) represent limitations for the IR. Fewer people think that defining what to report, to whom, and why is another limitation, as well as determining material non-financial issues, quantifying human, social or intellectual capitals, having no standards for IR, or restrictions from legislation. This question has the same response degree as the previous one.

Research Area (5) Determinants of Integrated Reporting

The next research theme concerns the topic of determinants of integrated report. The majority of those who replied our survey consider that organizations publish IR for marketing and corporate image but also for showing transparency. Then, companies are self – motivated to adopt IR because of the external benefits in terms of reputation and internal advantages of cost reduction. Finally, the economic factors has highest influence on the issuance of IR.

Regarding the next open question on why do organizations publish these IR, 28% of accountants answered that marketing and corporate image, stakeholders, promoting goodwill, transparency, mandatory regulation, and obtaining a competitive advantage are the main drivers of IR. Although having a low response rate, the question is useful for identifying the most

Table 25.

No.	Question	Type	Response Rate
Q32.	What are the limitations of IR?	CLOSED	
(no answer)		47	68%
A1	restrictions from legislation	1	1%
A2	the costs of preparing these reports: the need for specialists; coordination of financial and non-financial information between departments;	11	16%
A3	having no standards for IR	3	4%
A4	defining what to report, to whom, and why	4	6%
A5	determining material non-financial issues	2	3%
A6	quantifying human, social or intellectual capitals	1	1%
TOTAL RESPONDENTS		69	100%

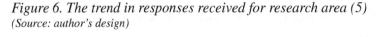

Figure 6. The trend in responses received for research area (5)
(Source: author's design)

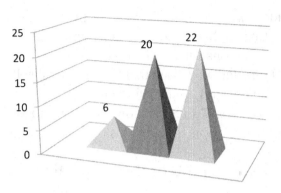

For a more accurate representation see the electronic version.

Table 26.

No.	Question	Type	Response Rate
Q11.	Why do you believe organizations publish these IR?	OPEN	28%
(no answer)		50	72%
A1	due to marketing and corporate image	6	9%
A2	for stakeholders	2	3%
A3	promoting goodwill	1	1%
A4	transparency reasons	6	9%
A5	mandatory by law	1	1%
A6	to obtain a competitive advantage	1	1%
A7	to obtain a competitive advantage/transparency	2	3%
TOTAL RESPONDENTS		69	100%

important determinants of an IR adoption from the perspective of the Romanian accountancy profession.

The following question seeks to investigate if companies are self-motivated to publish IR or they do it for marketing/image purposes. 32% agree that companies are self – motivated to adopt IR because of the external benefits in terms of reputation and internal advantages of cost reduction, while 20% believe corporations practice IR for marketing/image purposes. The response rate is more than 50%.

29% of accountants mention that the economic factor is the main external force that should influence the issuance of IR as an organization reporting

Table 27.

No.	Question	Type	Response Rate
Q12.	Do you think companies are self- motivated to publish these reports or they do it for marketing/image purposes (other reasons- please mention them)?	CLOSED	52%
(no answer)		33	48%
A1	I believe companies are self – motivated to adopt IR because of the external benefits in terms of reputation and internal advantages of cost reduction	22	32%
A2	I believe corporations practice IR for marketing/image purposes	14	20%
TOTAL RESPONDENTS		69	100%

Table 28.

No.	Question	Type	Response Rate
Q13.	Which of the following external forces should influence the issuance of IR as an organization reporting behaviour?	CLOSED	51%
(no answer)		34	49%
A1	political factors	2	3%
A2	economic factors	20	29%
A3	social factors	11	16%
A4	cultural factors	2	3%
TOTAL RESPONDENTS		69	100%

behavior. Next in line is the social factor (with 16% choices), while only 2 accounting specialists selected the political and cultural factors. This question was replied in more than 50% of the cases.

Research Area (6) Recommendations Concerning the IIRC Framework

The next category represents the recommendations on the IR framework. The most relevant feedback received indicated that none of the elements or principles from the IIRC framework should be added or excluded.

The next question refers to the elements of the IIRC Framework and has a low response rate – 25%. 14% of respondents agree that none of the content elements from the framework should be excluded. 6% would eliminate strategic

Figure 7. The trend in responses received for research area (6)
(Source: author's design)

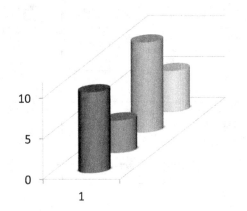

■ none of the elements from the IIRC framework should be excluded

■ none of the elements from the IIRC framework should be added

▨ none of the IIRC principles should be excluded

For a more accurate representation see the electronic version.

Table 29.

No.	Question	Type	Response Rate
Q15.	The IIRC framework is developed on a set of components (elements): organizational overview and business model; operating context, including risks and opportunities; strategic objectives and strategies to achieve those objectives; governance and remuneration; performance; future outlook. Which elements should be excluded from the framework and why?	OPEN	25%
(no answer)		52	75%
A1	depends on the target reader/stakeholder	1	1%
A2	governance and remuneration	1	1%
A3	governance and remuneration/ performance	1	1%
A4	None	10	14%
A5	strategic objectives and strategies to achieve those objectives- competition reasons	4	6%
TOTAL RESPONDENTS		69	100%

objectives and strategies to achieve those objectives from pure competition reasons, while few people would give up performance, governance and remuneration, and some would consider that it all depends on the target reader or stakeholder.

Regarding new elements that could be added to the framework, we did not receive much feedback (17% respondents only). People mentioned certain information that they would add in terms of human resources development,

Table 30.

No.	Question	Type	Response Rate
Q16.	What new elements should be added to the framework and why?	OPEN	17%
(no answer)		57	83%
A1	Details	1	1%
A2	human resources development	1	1%
A3	industry benchmarks, in order to help users grasp the performance of the organization compared to its peers.	1	1%
A4	more predictive elements - to show how the business will create value in the future	1	1%
A5	None	4	6%
A6	social and economical	2	3%
A7	I don't know	2	3%
TOTAL RESPONDENTS		69	100%

industry benchmarks - "to help users grasp the performance of the organization compared to its peers", more predictive elements –"to show how the business will create value in the future", as well as other social and economic information.

Furthermore, we investigated which principles should not be included in the framework, according to Romanian accountancy profession. The answer rate was in this case also low (22%). 11 accountants believe that none of the IIRC principles has to be excluded. Only 2 respondents think that stakeholder inclusiveness can be eliminated from the framework, while just one member of professional accounting associations considers strategic focus and future orientation (the latter "for keeping inside the competitive advantage").

The following question refers to new principles that could be added to the framework. The low response rate (17%) shows that completeness and an "easy to use" approach can enhance IR value, and ethical behavior should also be reported, also suggesting that the IIRC principles may be subject to legal requirements. Transparency was another element mentioned by the respondents that can be added to the list of principles.

Research Area (7) the Industry

The questions related to industry reveal that all corporations have a certain impact on society, no matter their activity sector, but still most of respondents agree that agree IIRC framework should be adapted to each sector. The

Table 31.

No.	Question	Type	Response Rate
Q17.	The IIRC framework contains also a set of principles: strategic focus; connectivity of information; future orientation; responsiveness and stakeholder inclusiveness; conciseness, reliability and materiality. Which principles should be excluded from the framework and why?	OPEN	22%
(no answer)		54	78%
A1	future orientation for keeping inside the competitive advantage	1	1%
A2	stakeholder inclusiveness	2	3%
A3	strategic focus	1	1%
A4	None	11	16%
TOTAL RESPONDENTS		69	100%

Table 32.

No.	Question	Type	Response Rate
Q18.	What new principles should be added to the framework and why?	OPEN	17%
(no answer)		57	83%
A1	completeness and Easy to Use - these should enhance the IR value	1	1%
A2	Details	1	1%
A3	ethics- all the principles mentioned above may be borderline to legal requirements; ethical behavior is a step higher.	1	1%
A4	I don't know	2	3%
A5	None	5	7%
A6	Transparency	2	3%
TOTAL RESPONDENTS		69	100%

interpretation would be that in respondents' view, all organizations have to report on a set of disclosure items, because even if the impact is lower, it cannot be eliminated (e.g. a bank may not have a direct impact upon the environment, but they can ask additional environmental information to a borrower who activates in the mining industry for instance).

30% of the Romanian professional accountants believe that all corporations have a certain impact on society and should be held accountable. The reply was for 32% from the 69 people.

In addition, 11 practitioners – against the same response rate as the previous- agreed that IIRC framework has to be adapted to each sector (for

Figure 8. The trend in responses received for research area (7)
(Source: author's design)

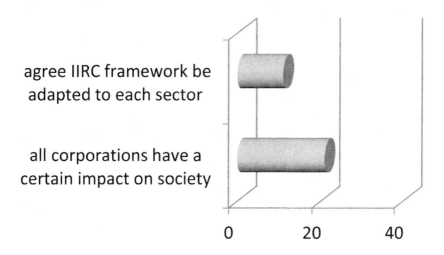

Table 33.

No.	Question	Type	Response Rate
Q36.	Do you believe that all companies should be held accountable in front of society?	CLOSED	32%
(no answer)		47	68%
A1	no, only some high- impact industries (e.g. chemical/oil and gas etc)	1	1%
A2	yes, all corporations have a certain impact on society	21	30%
TOTAL RESPONDENTS		69	100%

instance banks and insurance companies are less harmful to environment than chemical companies):

- "Given the high variety of business and the current lack of standards regarding this matter, there should be some customization applied for IR in different business sectors."
- "If the framework will be the same for everybody (banks vs. oil), then for some companies the IR will be a burden in terms of time and costs."
- However, some practitioners support the idea of a general framework for all industries:

- "You can harm the society by collapsing the entire financial sector in one country: your imprudence can lead to as much damage as any other industry".
- "They all have an impact: an insurance company that has low prices on insurance policies for old cars may influence the number of old cars that are used, and thus the impact on the environment is greater".

Research Area (8) Characteristics for IR Information

Regarding IR information characteristics, there is a majority of 21 people replying that relevance means that the respective information is important for

Table 34.

No.	Question	Type	Response Rate
Q37.	Should the IIRC framework be adapted to each sector? (e.g. banks and insurance companies are less harmful to environment than chemical companies).	CLOSED	32%
(no answer)		47	68%
A1	I agree	11	16%
A2	I strongly disagree	2	3%
A3	I strongly agree	6	9%
A4	I neither agree nor disagree	2	3%
A5	I disagree	1	1%
TOTAL RESPONDENTS		69	100%

Figure 9. The trend in responses received for research area (8)
(Source: author's design)

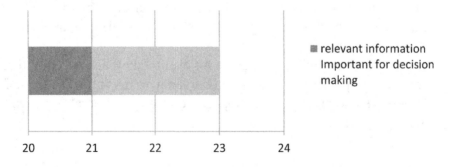

relevant information
Important for decision making

decision-making processes, while only 2 respondents managed to provide a definition for materiality as depending on the types of stakeholders/ sector/ financial and non-financial data.

Most of the professional accountants classified the relevant information as being important for decision making, critical for strategies and forecasts (30% of respondents), while 9 accounting specialists linked the term to the principle of going concern, conveying credibility for future projects, providing a fateful and updated business perspective, performance, or risk impacts and 6 respondents considered that this is just the equivalent of accounting information characteristic, being consistent, timely, material, comparable, clear and verifiable. Some practitioners presented general definitions, other perceive the relevant information as the totality of non-financial information (composed from social, environmental, and CSR information), or as the mixture between financial and non- financial elements. The most complex definition on relevant information was the following:

...Relevant information has significance whether it is financial or non-financial because it has a significant impact on the organization. Such examples are: information about employees (e.g. employee turnover, hiring process, fidelity bonuses for employees), information about the position of the product on the market, information about the evolutions in the industry in which the company activates, tax policies, events with significance in the social responsibility area...

The question had a response rate of over 50%.

58 people chosen not to answer at our question on IR materiality. The 11 accountants that did reply identified the following type of information as material for IR: financial, non-financial, performance, governance, profit/ pollution, employment/fired people, cost for reducing pollution. As additional remarks, threshold should be established for financial information and judgment applied for non - financial (assess the potential impact) and the information depends on stakeholders, industry, and company assessment. However, the response rate for IR materiality is low: 16%.

Table 35.

No.	Question	Type	Response Rate
Q3.	What do you understand by relevant information?	OPEN	62%
(no answer)		26	38%
A1	all financial and non- financial information	2	3%
A2	Important for decision making	21	30%
A3	non- financial information	2	3%
A4	going concern	9	13%
A5	general definition	3	4%
A6	linked to the one of the accounting information characteristics*	6	9%
TOTAL RESPONDENTS		69	100%

Table 36.

No.	Question	Type	Response Rate
Q38.	What information should be material for an IR?	OPEN	16%
(no answer)		58	84%
A1	dependent on the types of stakeholders	2	3%
A2	depends on the sector	2	3%
A3	depends on the company assessment	1	1%
A4	financial	1	1%
A5	financial and non-financial	2	3%
A6	performance, governance	1	1%
A7	profit/pollution, employment/fired people, cost for reducing pollution	1	1%
A8	threshold should be established for financial information and judgment applied for non - financial (assess the potential impact)	1	1%
TOTAL RESPONDENTS		69	100%

Research Area (9) Voluntary vs. Mandatory IR and Assurance

The last research theme involves a discussion on voluntary versus mandatory IR and its assurance. 17% consider that it would be better to promote a voluntary integrated reporting instead of a mandatory one, while 14% argue that corporate reporting environment needs a global standard for IR. 22% of

Figure 10. The trend in responses received for research area (9)
(Source: author's design)

■ IR should bevoluntary

■ it is too early to consider the assurance on IR

corporate reporting environment need a global standard for IR

■ IASB- FASB is most suitable for issuing a standard for IR

For a more accurate representation see the electronic version.

the answers qualified IASB- FASB as the most suitable for issuing a standard in the field of IR. Finally, 17% of the respondents think are not in favor of IR assurance at the moment.

The majority of professional accountants consider that IR should be voluntary and not mandatory because:

- "The option to do the report will enhance their quality."
- "Companies need to understand its principles in order to value them; making it mandatory can mean companies will follow a checklist approach without really trusting the benefits."

The ones who think that there is a need for mandatory IR, provide arguments for their choice also:

- "It will create a standard and everybody will compete equally"
- "All entities have an impact on society and their stakeholders in genera for transparency purposes."
- If is voluntary "it will be applied mostly by large corporations…"

Most of the patricians think that it is too early to talk about assurance of IR (at a 23% response rate), as "it will be accepted with difficulty by companies" and "this will rise more costs and the companies are still complaining about IR costs".

Table 37.

No.	Question	Type	Response Rate
Q39.	Integrated Reporting should be:	CLOSED	32%
(no answer)		47	68%
A1	voluntary	12	17%
A2	mandatory	10	14%
TOTAL RESPONDENTS		69	100%

Table 38.

No.	Question	Type	Response Rate
Q40.	Do you believe it is too early to consider the assurance, perhaps via some kind of independent 'audit' report, of IR?	CLOSED	23%
(no answer)		53	77%
A1	Yes	12	17%
A2	No	4	6%
TOTAL RESPONDENTS		69	100%

Table 39.

No.	QUESTION	Type	Response Rate
Q41.	Does the corporate reporting environment need a global STANDARD for IR?	CLOSED	32%
(no answer)		47	68%
A1	I agree	9	13%
A2	I strongly agree	10	14%
A3	I neither agree nor disagree	3	4%
TOTAL RESPONDENTS		69	100%

28% of the accountancy profession members agreed that corporate reporting environment need a global standard for IR from the following reasons:

- "In this way the reports are comparable, regardless of the country in which the company operates".

Table 40.

No.	Question	Type	Response Rate
Q42.	Which policy makers/professional bodies/members of professional bodies is more suitable for issuing such a standard?	CLOSED	32%
(no answer)		47	68%
A1	GRI	1	1%
A2	IASB- FASB	15	22%
A3	IIRC	6	9%
TOTAL RESPONDENTS		69	100%

- "There should be a standard to help develop a proper structure of the reporting, and to reduce the impact of issues such as deciding which information to report."

The majority of the respondents (22%) believe that IASB- FASB is the most suitable for issuing a standard on integrated reporting. Some consider the IIRC is the proper accounting professional body for issuing such standards (9%), while only one respondent selected GRI as the main driver for these standards. Other potential standard developers are the state governments.

Summary of Findings for Research Areas 4-9

The second research question refers to the information that should be included in an integrated report and the reasons that determine this choice. According to the opinion of accountancy profession, the principles and elements from the IIRC Framework should remain the same, while there is a need to adapt this framework to each industry sector. The information from the integrated report has to target the investor- as main audience, while of course its outcomes regard also the other stakeholders, including the clients and society. The main challenge faced by the integrated report remains the cost of collecting and presenting the information to enhance reporting transparency. Regarding the reasons why companies choose to include certain type of information in the report or issue integrated reports, we found that organizations publish IR for marketing and corporate image and transparency reasons. However, the majority of respondents consider that companies are self – motivated to adopt IR because of the external benefits in terms of reputation and internal advantages of cost reduction, while the economic factor is another determinant for the issuance of IR. In addition, the information included in the IR should be relevant for decision-making and material (for stakeholders, sector, financial and non-financial data). Finally, for a better understanding and assessment of the information from the integrated report, we need both standards for IR and assurance. The perspective of accountancy profession is that IR has to be applied on a voluntary basis, although IR needs a global standard that could be issued by IASB- FASB.

Regarding assurance, it is too early to consider the assurance for IR.

Finally, we received an interesting comment from one of the respondents who sustains that integrated reporting will be hard to apply in Eastern Europe. We agree with this statement as countries from this part of Europe have less- developed economies or in the best case represent emergent economies. They were somehow left behind the developed countries because of the communism period and is more difficult for them to adapt to new corporate reporting trends and shifts from traditional reporting to modern reporting tools and techniques, such as IR.

Within the next section, we are going to discuss the results for the empirical analysis on the framework prototype development, from the second part of our research.

Figure 8 presents an example of data centralization in excel. The frequency contained in the disclosure index represents the total apparition of the elements from the framework. The frequency value was returned, as mentioned before, by Tropes semantic software that was programmed to counts the apparition for each IR element. The minimum value of the frequency was 0 (when the annual report did not mention the specific information at all). We do not have a maximum interval, as the number of apparition shows the disclosure degree for the elements in our framework (the higher this degree, the more integrated will that report become).

Further on, Figures 11- 13 provide a clear view on data gathering for specific elements in our framework, per year of analysis. The excel database was completed after the annual reports were processed, one by one, though Tropes software. Each search in Tropes generated one Tropes report on frequencies, so we had to centralize all the data extracted from the software analysis in a single file for all the 5 years.

Finally, we had to upload the data into SPSS and run statistical tests to show the evolution of IR disclosure and the impact that organizational characteristics and country- level indicators have on IR. The data has been processed using SPSS13 (Statistical Package for the Social Sciences) for

Figure 11. Data centralization in Microsoft excel for year 2009
(Source: from excel centralized database- author's design)

Crt. Nr	Organization	Df - measured as sum of disclosure frequencies					Price per share					Market value				
		2009	2010	2011	2012	2013	2009	2010	2011	2012	2013	2009	2010	2011	2012	2013
14	Agilent Technologies	-	124	145	131	131	11,4271	24,7134	32,3862	32,0144	29,7047	-	-	-	-	-
15	Airgas	-	90	78	95	77	37,11	63,67	67,44	89,88	95,95	3.017,82	5.267,39	5.677,62	6.863,61	7.284,26
16	Ajinomoto	-	10	14	75	4	-	-	-	-	-	4.923,59	6.614,83	7.112,58	8.539,80	8.920,33
17	Akzo Nobel	-	-	-	842	1087	41,2156	58,4113	71,4919	55,2153	60,9425	10.691,76	13.531,78	16.562,09	12.958,38	14.518,49
18	Alcatel-Lucent	-	632	1215	1047	-	-	-	-	-	-	5.151,02	7.324,58	13.491,15	4.961,53	3.312,43
19	Alcoa	-	200	208	227	-	7,91	15,03	18,13	9,63	8,24	7.517,00	15.334,77	19.266,52	10.271,30	8.811,66
20	All Nippon Airways	-	0	348	459	465	3,34	4,41	3,75	3,73	4,82	3.551,36	4.679,88	3.979,11	3.959,28	5.116,35
21	Alliance Data Systems	-	528	470	-	464	-	-	-	-	-	2.345,53	3.466,97	4.301,08	6.325,95	7.747,99
22	Alliance One Internation	-	-	182	184	182	3,89	5,41	4,08	3,52	3,74	346,11	481,97	355,31	307,55	327,78
23	Allianz	-	1408	1187	-	-	92,579	127,69	145,896	112,351	137,631	41.943,01	57.958,34	66.309,78	51.153,34	62.752,84
24	Allstate	-	757	711	1019	-	20,54	32,62	31,65	32,75	49,32	11.010,29	17.530,21	16.628,87	16.161,96	23.082,45
25	Alstom	-	1050	1136	-	-	56,8532	63,4434	63,7014	36,562	39,7428	16.319,59	18.633,88	18.752,09	10.768,06	12.242,27
26	American Eagle Outfitter	-	94	95	144	101	-	-	-	-	-	-	-	-	-	-
27	Amerigroup	-	25	16	69	-	28,47	34,31	62,92	67,45	91,7	1.512,21	1.771,21	3.116,18	3.245,37	4.695,76
28	AmerisourceBergen	-	23	37	37	51	16,405	29,03	40,57	38,22	52,08	4.996,24	8.197,58	11.120,01	9.854,42	11.987,39
29	Amgen	-	252	253	-	-	47,84	60,29	54,08	68,02	104,04	49.464,81	58.574,93	50.412,83	53.123,60	77.959,38
30	Anixter International	-	90	0	101	-	32,29	47,66	71,8	70,71	68,51	1.134,31	1.603,35	2.473,43	2.348,96	2.225,17
31	AOL	-	-	-	203	- (NA)	NA	26,39	20,53	18,42	38,62	NA	2.811,44	2.195,13	1.715,01	2.981,91
32	Apple	-	-	164	144	150	16,9214	34,22	48,2914	90,5257	60,4571	105.486,10	217.213,50	311.428,60	592.479,30	397.847,60
34	Applied Materials	-	-	220	288	261	11,56	13,48	15,75	12,03	13,2	-	-	-	-	-
36	Arrow Electronics	-	101	120	248	240	-	-	-	-	-	2.342,56	3.658,50	4.977,83	4.537,80	4.063,65
37	Assicurazioni Generali	-	-	1015	1487	-	-	-	-	-	-	24.725,70	37.754,91	35.582,35	22.451,72	24.794,43
38	Association of Chartered	28	63	138	208	-	-	-	-	-	-	-	-	-	-	-
39	AstraZeneca	1025	1257	1050	1439	-	35,14	44,38	47,77	43,96	50,39	50.872,84	64.330,40	66.112,00	55.982,22	62.973,47
40	AT&T	127	135	97	104	-	26,59	26,31	30,47	30,94	38,02	156.703,00	155.283,50	180.121,20	181.772,40	208.790,80

Figure 12. Data centralization in Microsoft excel for year 2010
(Source: from excel centralized database- author's design)

Crt. No.	Organization	Mission	Vision	Strategy	Business Model	Performance	Governance	Future outlook	Opportunities	Risks	Report preparation	Report presentation	Strategic focus	Future orientation	Connectivity of information
291	Qualcomm			1	2	2			3	1					
292	Quanta Computer			1		1									
293	Quest Diagnostics	1		14		67	21		19	72					
294	Randstad Holding	8	2	49	1	141	25		26	139					
295	Raytheon	58	7	36		118	10		12	74				1	
296	Reckitt Benckiser Group		1	20	2	119	16		5	102				1	
297	Regions Financial		1	27	1	56	8		4	333					
298	Reliance Steel & Aluminum			10	1	30	2		11	49					
299	Renault	3	13	24	4	52	18		4	10					
300	Repsol, S.A		3	33	1	14	2		6	33					
301	Research In Motion			5		11	10		3	39					
302	Reynolds American			25	1	31	21		3	55					
303	Ricoh	5	5	6	3	13	5		6	42					
304	Rio Tinto		10	110	2	354	148		41	178					
305	Robert Bosch	3	9	17		9	1		15	81					
306	RockTenn			10		46	11		5	48					
307	Rockwell Automation Inc	1	2	19	1	42	4		14	56					
308	Rosneft	1		23		100	85		3	111					
309	Ross Stores	1		25	4	29	3		5	18					
310	Royal Ahold	1	11	42	4	99	27		23	680				1	
311	ROYAL BANK OF CA	1	11	42	4	99	27		23	680				1	

Figure 13. Data centralization in Microsoft excel for year 2011
(Source: from excel centralized database- author's design)

Crt. No	Organization	Present obligation	Outflow of resource	Reasonable estimate	Commitment to transpar	obligation to society	reputation risk	Commitment to investors	Environmental Informat	Social information	Employee-related Informat	respect of human rights	anti-corruption	bribery	Age	Gender
85	Cisco Systems															3
86	Citigroup				3								3	1	13	
87	Cliffs Natural Resour														12	
88	Clorox															
89	CLP Holdings Limited	10	2												2	
90	CNP Assurances											5	1	1	4	2
91	Coach															1
92	Coca-Cola											58	12	8	11	13
93	Coca-Cola İçecek AS	1	2												1	
94	Coega Development		1													1
95	Cognizant Technolog												2		1	
96	Colgate-Palmolive														15	
97	Collective Brands														5	
98	Comcast			1											4	3
99	Commonwealth Bank	2		1											15	
100	CommScope														3	2
101	Community Health Sy															
102	Compagnie de Saint-(		1									2		1	6	
103	Compal Electronics															
104	Corning			3											11	
105	Corporate Social Res					2						6	1			5
106	Costco Wholesale			1											2	1
107	CPA Australia Ltd											1	3	1	4	17
108	CPN														26	1

Figure 14. Data centralization in Microsoft excel for year 2012
(Source: from excel centralized database- author's design)

Crt. No	Organization	Discrimination	Disciplinary Practices	Working Hours	Remuneration	Management Systems	Inclusivity	Materiality	Responsiveness	Integrate with governance	Integrate with organizational strategy and	Purpose of stakeholder engagement
118	Darden Restaurants, Inc.											
119	DaVita											
120	Dean Foods											
121	Deere						1					
122	Deloitte LLP				10							1
123	Deloitte Netherlands	1			4							7
124	Delta Air Lines											
125	Delta Lloyd Group	1		1	104		2			1		2
126	Denso				8		1					
127	Det Norske Veritas Ltd	1			9		1					5
128	Deutsche Bank				27		2					
129	Deutsche Lufthansa AG	3			75	5						
130	Deutsche Post (DHL)	1			88							
131	Devon Energy											
132	Diageo											
133	Dillard's	2										
134	Discover Financial Services	1										
135	Discovery Communications											
136	DNV Business Assurance	1			9		1					5
137	Dollar General				1		2					
138	Domtar											
139	Dongfeng Motor				50		1					
140	Doosan Infracore Co Ltd											
141	DTE Energy											

Figure 15. Data centralization in Microsoft excel for year 2013
(Source: from excel centralized database- author's design)

Crt. No.	Organization	Disciplinary Practices	Working Hours	Remuneration	Management Systems	Inclusivity	Materiality	Responsiveness	Integrate with governance	Integrate with organizational strategy and operations management	Purpose of stakeholder engagement	Stakeholder identification	Profile and map stakeholders	Determine engagement level and method	Sum of frequencies
130	Denso			8	1										127
131	Det Norske Veritas L			9	1							5			230
132	Deutsche Bank			27	2										2025
133	Deutsche Lufthansa A			75	5										685
134	Deutsche Post (DHL)			88											556
135	Devon Energy														113
136	Diageo														960
137	Dillard's														61
138	Discover Financial Se														485
139	Discovery Communic														192
140	DnB NOR		1	126	7										1016
141	DNV Business Assura			9	1							5			230
142	Dollar General			1	2										603
143	Dontar														220
144	Dongfeng Motor			50	1										160
145	Doosan Infracore Co														64
146	DTE Energy														39

Windows. Statistical tests were chosen considering the criteria of data characteristics or data structure and include descriptive statistics (means, std. Dev, std.Error, 95%CI, Min, Max), Kolmogorov-Smirnov, Sidack and Anova. The next two sections present the results obtained through SPSS data processing and of course, their interpretation.

Results SPSS Part 1: Analyzing the Behavior of IR Disclosure Index Elements

This section of the empirical investigation considers the first 10 elements from the IR disclosure index (mission, vision, strategy, business model, performance, governance, future outlook, opportunities, risks, report preparation)[1] as subject for statistical tests: Kolmogorov-Smirnov, Chi-square, Sidack test, and Anova.

At first, we centralized the data for the 10 elements from the IR scale. Then, the following two statistical hypotheses have been tested to investigate the IR evolution on disclosing that specific item:

H$_{01}$: The disclosure level of IR does not register significant changes from one year to another.

H$_{02}$: The disclosure level of IR registers significant changes from one year to another.

After investigating the evolution in time, we will pass to an analysis upon companies' reporting behavior in a specific year. This particular analysis takes place for each of the five years included in the study. Therefore, we have performed the Chi-square test[2] five times, starting from the next two hypothesis:

H$_{03}$: There is no discrepancy in the level of disclosure for specific IR elements between companies.

H$_{04}$: There are significant differences between the levels of disclosure for specific IR elements between companies.

The table below presents a summary of data distribution for the disclosure level of organization's mission as an element of IR. The disclosure levels were measured between companies' reports per year. Thus, the higher maximum levels were met for 2011 and 2012 (frequency of 77), while in 2013 we have at most 34 frequency score.

Below you can find the distribution of the disclosure level of the mission as an element of IR scale. The highest level for disclosure on organization's mission was registered in 2011, followed by 2012, 2009, 2010 and 2013.

The values representing disclosure on mission were included in a Kolmogorov-Smirnov test (p = 0.200), the data showing a normal distribution. Therefore, we went on and applied the Anova test (F = 0.753, p = 0.000)

Table 41. Descriptive analysis of data- Centralized indicators for disclosure on mission

	Mean	Std. Deviation	Std. Error	95% Confidence Interval for Mean		Minimum	Maximum
				Lower Bound	Upper Bound		
2009	2.55	6.488	.310	1.94	3.16	0	70
2010	2.54	6.119	.277	2.00	3.09	0	70
2011	2.73	6.424	.296	2.15	3.31	0	77
2012	2.66	6.329	.295	2.08	3.24	0	77
2013	2.17	4.511	.283	1.62	2.73	0	34
Total	2.57	6.142	.134	2.30	2.83	0	77

(Source: SPSS data processing)

Discussion of Results

Figure 16. Frequency for disclosure on organizational mission
(Source: SPSS data processing)

Crt. No	Organization	Materiality	Responsiveness	Integrate with governance	Integrate with organizational strategy and	Purpose of stakeholder engagement	Stakeholder identification	Profile and map stakeholders	Determine engagement level and meth	Sum of frequencies
184	SFN Group									25
185	Shimizu									44
186	Shree Cement Limited						2			323
187	Sime Darby Berhad						22			430
188	Smithfield Foods						1			87
189	Sompo Japan Insurance						1			251
190	Sonoco Products									186
191	Spectrum Brands									207
192	Sprint									558
193	Stanley Black & Decker									23
194	Starbucks									143
195	State Farm Insurance									2
196	Steelcase									188
197	STMicroelectronics									511
198	Stockland	2			4				7	376
199	Stora Enso	4			3			8		445
200	Sumitomo Chemical									239
201	Sumitomo Electric Industri									120
202	SunTrust Banks									713
203	Swiss Reinsurance				1					1160
204	Syngenta AG							1		346
205	T. Rowe Price									91
206	Tata Steel							1		304
207	Telefónica									683

Figure 17. Mean values for disclosure frequency on mission
(Source: SPSS data processing)

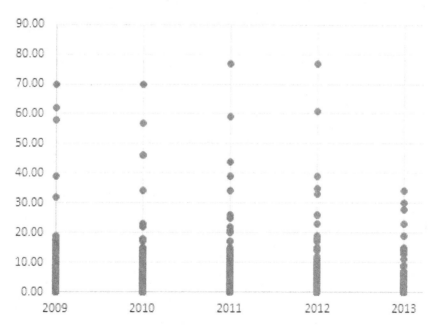

73

that rejects the null hypothesis accepting the alternative one, which is the fact that indeed the disclosure level of IR registers significant changes from one year to another from the perspective of mentioning and explaining the organizational mission.

Applying the Sidack test (p = 0.000) we arrive to the same conclusion that IR disclosure on company's mission registers significant changes from one year to another.

The Chi-square test has been run for each year of our analysis, generating similar results that sustain the 4th hypothesis[3], proving that companies register significant differences between the levels of disclosure for specific IR elements (information on mission).

Now, we will pass to the second IR disclosure item: organizational vision. As in the previous case, we start by presenting the centralized indicators:

In 2011 companies register the highest frequency for disclosure on organizational vision, followed by 2012, 2009, 2010 and 2013 (Chart no. 3):

The Kolmogorov-Smirnov (p = 0.200) test shows that data is normally distributed for the frequencies on organizational vision disclosure. After applying Anova test F = 363.219, p = 0.000 we can reject the null hypothesis and accept the alternative one: the disclosure level of IR registers significant changes from one year to another from the perspective of mentioning and explaining the vision of the company. This statement is also sustained through Sidack test (p = 0.000). We present the evolution of IR disclosure on vision in the chart below:

The results obtained for the Chi-Square test[4] sustain the 4th hypothesis: companies register significant differences between the level of disclosure for specific IR elements (information on vision).

Table 42. Descriptive analysis of data- Centralized indicators for disclosure on vision

	Mean	Std. Deviation	Std. Error	95% Confidence Interval for Mean		Minimum	Maximum
				Lower Bound	Upper Bound		
2009	3.00	5.723	.018	2.96	3.04	0	52
2010	3.39	6.749	.022	3.35	3.43	0	69
2011	8.08	72.630	.232	7.63	8.54	0	1167
2012	3.18	5.929	.018	3.15	3.22	0	57
2013	3.59	6.660	.037	3.52	3.66	0	45
Total	4.34	35.163	.054	4.23	4.44	0	1167

(Source: SPSS data processing)

Figure 18. Frequency for disclosure on organizational vision
(Source: SPSS data processing)

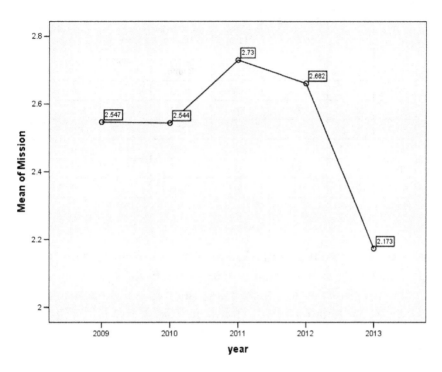

Figure 19. Mean values for disclosure frequency on vision
(Source: SPSS data processing)

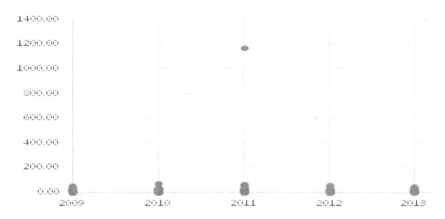

Table 43. Descriptive analysis of data- Centralized indicators for disclosure on strategy

		Mean	Std. Deviation	Std. Error	95% Confidence Interval for Mean		Minimum	Maximum
					Lower Bound	Upper Bound		
Strategy	2009	25.19	25.622	.083	25.03	25.35	0	213
	2010	27.58	29.954	.096	27.39	27.77	0	243
	2011	27.23	30.508	.097	27.04	27.42	0	239
	2012	30.27	35.143	.108	30.06	30.48	0	312
	2013	33.69	35.187	.196	33.31	34.08	0	285
	Total	28.10	31.086	.047	28.00	28.19	0	312

(Source: SPSS data processing)

The next item from the IR disclosure index is information on company's strategy. The table below contains the descriptive statistics:

Kolmogorov-Smirnov test (p = 0.200) showed a normal distribution of data, so we went on and applied Anova analysis (F = 631.097, p = 0.000) that rejects the null hypothesis and accepts the alternative hypothesis: IR disclosure on company's strategy registers significant changes from one year to another.

Through Sidack test (p = 0.000) we measured the medium frequency per year and try to identify if there are differences between time periods:

During all the five years we found that companies register significant differences between the level of disclosure for specific IR elements (information on strategy) as the Chi- Square test showed the following values: Chi-Square = 238.260, p = 0.000 (2009), Chi-Square = 344.099, p = 0.000 (2010), Chi-Square = 119.802, p = 0.000 (2011), Chi-Square = 164.068, p = 0.000 (2012), Chi-Square = 184.299, p = 0.000 (2013). The following chart presents the frequency distribution per year of the disclosure levels for information on company's strategy.

As we can observe from the chart, in 2013 the level of information disclosure for company's strategy is the highest, followed by 2013, 2010, 2011 and 2009.

Concerning the disclosure levels for business model, we present again the centralized data:

Kolmogorov-Smirnov test (p = 0.200) indicates a normal distribution of data, thus we could apply Anova (F = 621.768, p = 0.000), the results validating the 2nd hypothesis: IR disclosure on company's business model

Figure 20. Mean values for disclosure frequency on strategy
(Source: SPSS data processing)

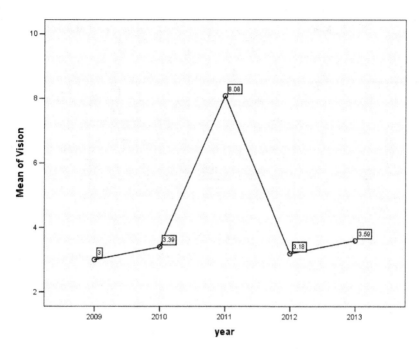

Figure 21. Frequency for disclosure on organizational strategy
(Source: SPSS data processing)

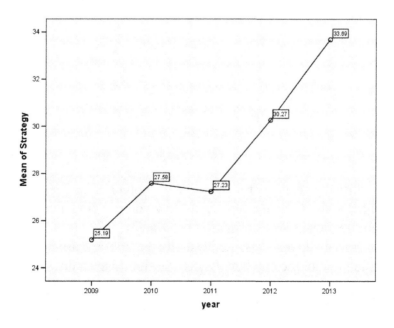

Table 44. Descriptive analysis of data- Centralized indicators for disclosure on business model

		Mean	Std. Deviation	Std. Error	95% Confidence Interval for Mean		Minimum	Maximum
					Lower Bound	Upper Bound		
Business_ Model	2009	1.94	3.294	.011	1.92	1.96	0	28
	2010	2.01	3.723	.012	1.99	2.04	0	32
	2011	2.43	4.970	.016	2.40	2.46	0	57
	2012	2.66	5.401	.017	2.63	2.70	0	66
	2013	2.95	4.467	.025	2.90	3.00	0	57
	Total	2.32	4.476	.007	2.31	2.34	0	66

(Source: SPSS data processing)

Figure 22. Mean values for disclosure frequency on business model
(Source: SPSS data processing)

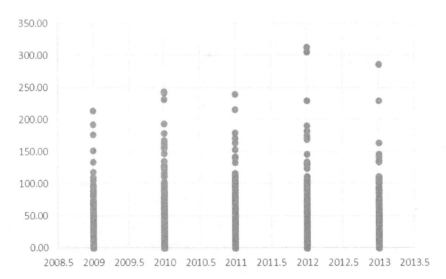

registers significant changes from one year to another. Sidack test (p = 0.004/ 0.000) confirms the same hypothesis. Below you can find a distribution of the medium frequency for information on strategy.

Going further to the year-based analysis, for the first time in our investigation we find validation for the null hypothesis: the significance threshold for Chi-Square test is over 0.05 in 2009: Chi-Square = 3.255, p = 0.075. Therefore, there is no change in the level of disclosure for specific IR elements (business model) between companies. As for the rest of the years from our analysis, the null hypothesis has been rejected and the alternative accepted: companies register significant differences between the level of disclosure for specific IR elements (information on business model). The results of the test assumed the following scores: in 2010 (Chi-Square = 384.857, p = 0.000), in 2011 (Chi-Square = 4.753, p = 0.029), in 2012 (Chi-Square = 95.596, p = 0.000), in 2013 (Chi-Square = 110.743, p = 0.000).

The maximum frequency of business model information disclosure was in 2012, followed by 2013, 2011, 2010 and 2009. The chart below shows the frequency distribution:

The main indicators on disclosure level for performance is showed in the table below:

Kolmogorov-Smirnov test (p = 0.200) indicates again that data is normally distributed. According to Anova (F = 1062.643, p = 0.000) the alternative hypothesis becomes true: IR disclosure on company's performance registers significant changes from one year to another. Sidack test (p = 0.000) shows the same result, emphasizing the following distribution for early medium frequency:

Figure 23. Frequency for disclosure on organizational business model
(Source: SPSS data processing)

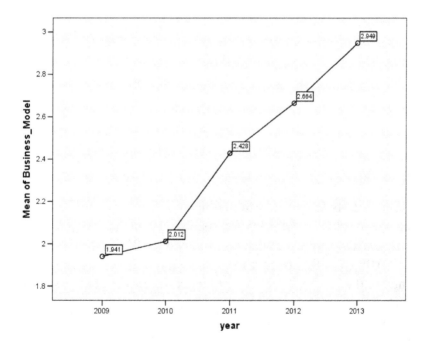

Table 45. Descriptive analysis of data- Centralized indicators for disclosure on performance

		Mean	Std. Deviation	Std. Error	95% Confidence Interval for Mean		Minimum	Maximum
					Lower Bound	Upper Bound		
Performance	2009	61.17	74.860	.242	60.70	61.64	0	519
	2010	65.77	75.053	.241	65.30	66.24	0	665
	2011	68.60	83.950	.268	68.07	69.13	0	553
	2012	77.50	94.975	.291	76.93	78.07	0	735
	2013	91.76	106.369	.591	90.60	92.92	0	795
	Total	70.26	85.374	.130	70.00	70.51	0	795

(Source: SPSS data processing)

Figure 24. Mean values for disclosure frequency on performance
(Source: SPSS data processing)

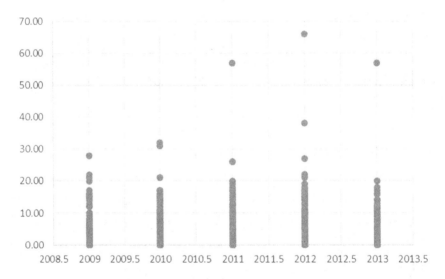

Chi-Square tests demonstrate that companies register significant differences between the level of disclosure for specific IR elements (information on performance), excepting for what we obtained in 2011 when the significance was over 0.05 (p = 0.086) and the null hypothesis was accepted: there is no change in the level of disclosure for specific IR elements (performance) between companies. The values resulted from the test were: 2009 (Chi-Square = 343.439, p = 0.000), 2010 (Chi-Square = 104.412, p = 0.000), 2011 (Chi-

Figure 25. Frequency for disclosure on organizational performance
(Source: SPSS data processing)

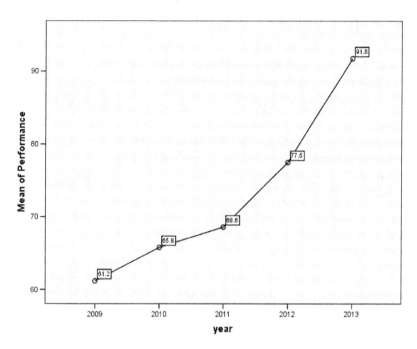

Table 46. Descriptive analysis of data- Centralized indicators for disclosure on governance

		Mean	Std. Deviation	Std. Error	95% Confidence Interval for Mean		Minimum	Maximum
					Lower Bound	Upper Bound		
Governance	2009	22.14	34.210	.111	21.92	22.36	0	256
	2010	24.41	40.124	.129	24.16	24.66	0	317
	2011	25.51	43.800	.140	25.23	25.78	0	320
	2012	27.13	45.517	.139	26.86	27.40	0	430
	2013	27.18	40.093	.223	26.74	27.62	0	424
	Total	25.04	41.232	.063	24.91	25.16	0	430

(Source: SPSS data processing)

Square = 2.942, p = 0.086), 2012 (Chi-Square = 784.846, p = 0.000), 2013 (Chi-Square = 0.023, p = 0.879).

The maximum point for disclosure on company's performance is registered in 2013, followed by 2012, 2010, 2011 and 2009:

Further on, we are going to detail the centralized indicators for governance:

The application of Kolmogorov-Smirnov test ($p = 0.200$) shows the normal distribution of data and allows for Anova statistical analysis ($F = 217.887$, $p = 0.000$) that proves the following statement: IR disclosure on company's governance registers significant changes from one year to another. Sidack test ($p = 0.000$) strengthens this interpretation. The medium frequencies on governance disclosure level (different from one year to another) can be found below:

The Chi-Square test reveals that the second null hypothesis is rejected and the alternative accepted: companies register significant differences between the levels of disclosure for specific IR elements (information on governance). The results per year were as follows: Chi-Square = 3.977, $p = 0.046$ (2009), Chi-Square = 72.193, $p = 0.000$ (2010), Chi-Square = 124.318, $p = 0.000$ (2011), Chi-Square = 141.462, $p = 0.000$ (2012), Chi-Square = 113.300, $p = 0.000$ (2013).

According to the frequency distribution (Chart 22), the highest levels of disclosure have been reached in 2012, followed by 2013, 2010, 2011 and 2009.

The descriptive statistics for future outlook – as an element of IR disclosure index is shown in the table below:

Figure 26. Mean values for disclosure frequency on governance
(Source: SPSS data processing)

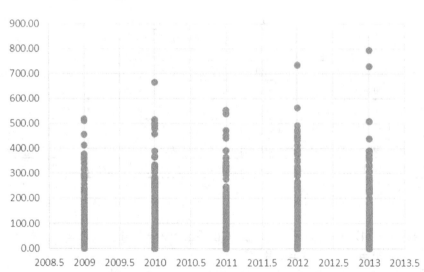

Figure 27. Frequency for disclosure on organizational governance
(Source: SPSS data processing)

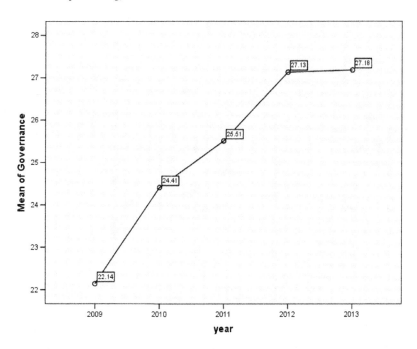

Table 47. Descriptive analysis of data- Centralized indicators for disclosure on future outlook

		Mean	Std. Deviation	Std. Error	95% Confidence Interval for Mean		Minimum	Maximum
					Lower Bound	Upper Bound		
Future_outlook	2009	.05	.392	.001	.05	.05	0	6
	2010	.01	.104	.000	.01	.01	0	5
	2011	.02	.136	.000	.02	.02	0	3
	2012	.10	.976	.003	.09	.10	0	17
	2013	.06	.323	.002	.06	.07	0	3
	Total	.05	.535	.001	.04	.05	0	17

(Source: SPSS data processing)

Figure 28. Mean values for disclosure frequency on future outlook
(Source: SPSS data processing)

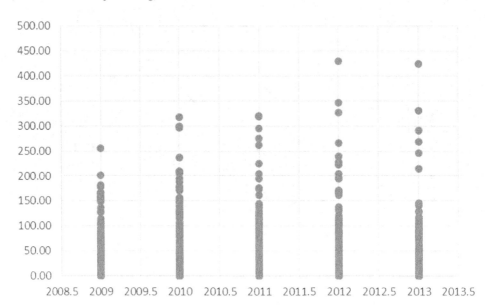

After applying Kolmogorov-Smirnov test (p = 0.200) the data presented a normal distribution. Anova test (F = 452.590, p = 0.000) shows that IR disclosure on company's future outlook registers significant changes from one year to another. Sidack test (p = 0.000) confirms this statement. The following chart contains the distribution medium frequencies for the analysed period:

Regarding the research on companies' behavior during a specific year, we found that in 2009 the null hypothesis is accepted (Chi-Square = 3.166, p = 0.075): there is no change in the level of disclosure for specific IR elements (future outlook) between companies. For the other years, Chi-Square indicates that companies register significant differences between the level of disclosure for specific IR elements (information on future outlook): Chi-Square = 837.653, p = 0.000 (2010), Chi-Square = 837.653, p = 0.000 (2011), Chi-Square = 73.639, p = 0.000 (2012), Chi-Square = 20.287, p = 0.000 (2013).

In 2013 the disclosure level for future outlook reaches its maximum, followed by 2009, 2010, 2011, and 2013:

The next element of the IR framework is opportunities. We provide below the descriptive statistics for this disclosure item.

Kolmogorov-Smirnov test that shows a normal data distribution (p = 0.200) permitted for further investigation though Anova analysis (F = 216.487, p

Figure 29. Frequency for disclosure on organizational future outlook
(Source: SPSS data processing)

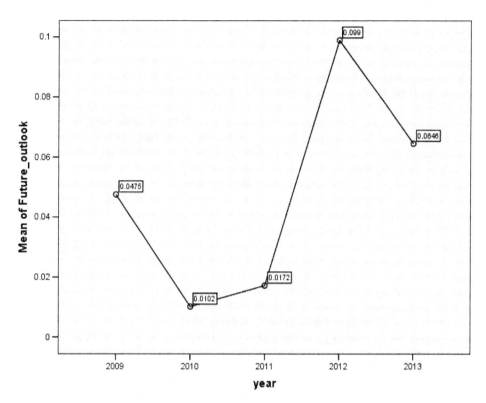

Table 48. Descriptive analysis of data- Centralized indicators for disclosure on opportunities

		Mean	Std. Deviation	Std. Error	95% Confidence Interval for Mean		Minimum	Maximum
					Lower Bound	Upper Bound		
Opportunities	2009	10.18	13.375	.043	10.09	10.26	0	122
	2010	10.25	11.642	.037	10.17	10.32	0	104
	2011	10.58	12.091	.039	10.50	10.65	0	122
	2012	11.26	12.487	.038	11.18	11.33	0	114
	2013	11.97	11.852	.066	11.84	12.10	0	118
	Total	10.69	12.384	.019	10.65	10.72	0	122

(Source: SPSS data processing)

85

Figure 30. Mean values for disclosure frequency on opportunities
(Source: SPSS data processing)

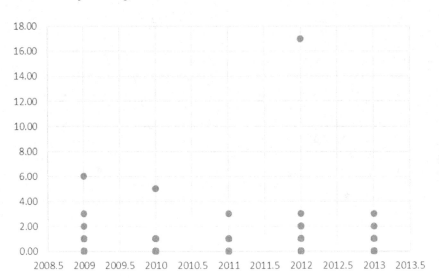

= 0.000). The results conducted to the alternative hypothesis: IR disclosure on company's opportunities registers significant changes from one year to another. Sidack test (p = 0.000) confirms this hypothesis also. The distribution of frequency means is as follows:

The Chi-Square test shows that companies register significant differences between the level of disclosure for specific IR elements (information on opportunities): Chi-Square = 28.842, p = 0.000 (2009), Chi-Square = 49.635, p = 0.000 (2010), Chi-Square = 98.75, p = 0.000 (2011), Chi-Square = 21.770, p = 0.000 (2012), Chi-Square = 141.031, p = 0.000 (2013). The highest disclosure frequency is met for year 2009, followed by 2011, 2013, 2012 and 2010:

The next element from the IR disclosure index is organizational risks. Table no. 10 presents the descriptive statistics for this item.

Kolmogorov-Smirnov test (p = 0.200) indicates that there is a normal distribution of data. After applying Anova test (F = 356.607, p = 0.000) we find that IR disclosure on company's risks registers significant changes from one year to another, that is also confirmed though Sidack test (p = 0.000/ 0.002). The frequency means distribution per years can be found below:

The Chi-Square test shows that companies register significant differences between the level of disclosure for specific IR elements (information on risks): Chi-Square = 1279.916, p = 0.000 (2009), Chi-Square = 373.261, p = 0.000

Figure 31. Frequency for disclosure on opportunities
(Source: SPSS data processing)

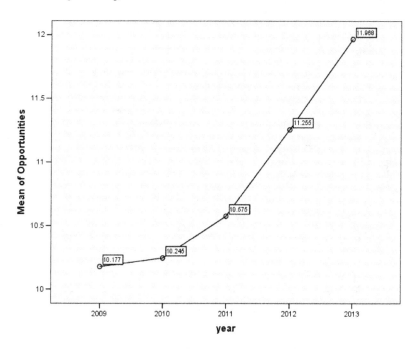

Table 49. Descriptive analysis of data- Centralized indicators for disclosure on risks

		Mean	Std. Deviation	Std. Error	95% Confidence Interval for Mean		Minimum	Maximum
					Lower Bound	Upper Bound		
Risks	2009	116.99	256.348	.829	115.37	118.62	0	3010
	2010	99.97	169.071	.543	98.90	101.03	0	1437
	2011	98.60	180.132	.576	97.47	99.73	0	1586
	2012	120.54	225.047	.690	119.19	121.89	0	2091
	2013	139.23	257.423	1.430	136.43	142.04	0	2762
	Total	111.51	214.950	.328	110.87	112.16	0	3010

(Source: SPSS data processing)

(2010), Chi-Square = 252.815, p = 0.000 (2011), Chi-Square = 940.433, p = 0.000 (2012), Chi-Square = 363.734, p = 0.000 (2013). The highest level of disclosure on risk related information appears in 2009:

The last item studies in this part of the analysis is the information on report preparation. We have below the descriptive statistics for this element:

Figure 32. Mean values for disclosure frequency on risks
(Source: SPSS data processing)

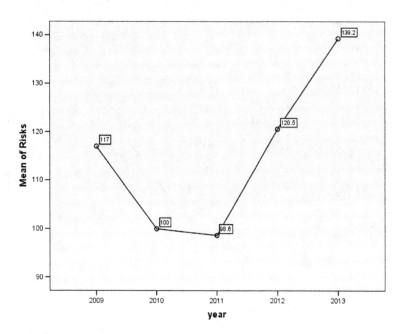

Figure 33. Frequency for disclosure on risks
(Source: SPSS data processing)

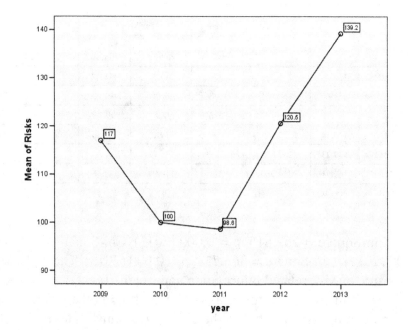

Table 51. Descriptive analysis of data- Centralized indicators for disclosure on report preparation

		Mean	Std. Deviation	Std. Error	95% Confidence Interval for Mean		Minimum	Maximum
					Lower Bound	Upper Bound		
Report_ preparation	2009	.01	.147	.000	.01	.01	0	2
	2010	.01	.114	.000	.01	.01	0	2
	2011	.01	.098	.000	.01	.01	0	1
	2012	.01	.124	.000	.01	.01	0	3
	2013	.01	.121	.001	.01	.01	0	2
	Total	.01	.122	.000	.01	.01	0	3

(Source: SPSS data processing)

The value obtained from Kolmogorov-Smirnov test (p = 0.200) highlights that data is normally distributed. Through Anova (F = 12.986, p = 0.000) and Sidack test (p = 0.001/ 0.000) we managed to validate the alternative

Figure 34. Mean values for disclosure frequency on report preparation
(Source: SPSS data processing)

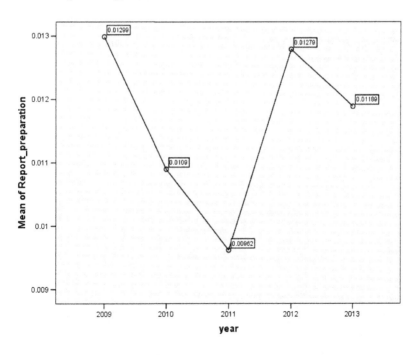

hypothesis: IR disclosure on report preparation registers significant changes from one year to another. The medium frequency per years is presented below:

According to the Chi-Square test, companies register significant differences between the level of disclosure for specific IR elements (report preparation): Chi-Square = 442.454, p = 0.000 (2009), Chi-Square = 569.231, p = 0.000 (2010), Chi-Square = 432.042, p = 0.000 (2011), Chi-Square = 1005.844, p = 0.000 (2012), Chi-Square = 488.161, p = 0.000 (2013).

In 2012, we have the maximum frequency for the disclosure level on report preparation:

Finally, we used the cluster analysis for investigating if there are differences between the corporations' reporting behavior:

H_{05}: There is no discrepancy between companies' reporting behavior in what regards the IR disclosure level.

H_{06}: There are discrepancies between companies' reporting behavior in what regards the IR disclosure level.

The cluster variable has been set as the companies' reporting behavior per year of analysis. In order to determine the models/ groups of companies with the same performance policy we applied the hierarchic method and the K-means methods of clustering. The performance scores have split the

Figure 35. Frequency for disclosure on report preparation
(Source: SPSS data processing)

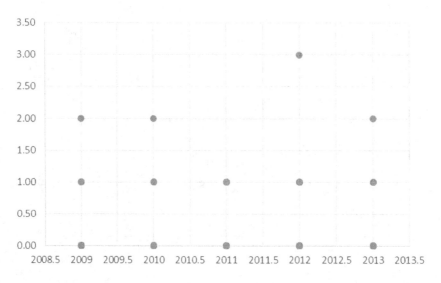

reporting behavior of companies in two main classes. The K-means algorithm generated two classes of homogenous groups, where the inter-class inertia value highly overcomes the values of intra-class inertia.

The results for F test on significance thresholds indicates that the elements/items of mission ($F = 68.422$, $p = 0.000$), vision ($F = 175.965$, $p = 0.000$), strategy ($F = 1088.261$, $p = 0.000$), business model ($F = 195.655$, $p = 0.000$), performance ($F = 814.850$, $p = 0.000$), governance ($F = 869.347$, $p = 0.000$), future outlook ($F = 6.227$, $p = 0.013$), opportunities ($F = 522.010$, $p = 0.000$), report preparation ($F = 210.357$ $p = 0.000$), future orientation ($F = 138.647$, $p = 0.000$) represent the main criteria for assigning the companies from our sample to clusters. At the other side, the elements/ items that did not have any influence in cluster creation were report presentation ($F = 3.273$, $p = 0.07$) and strategic focus ($F = 0.611$, $p = 0.435$).

The composition of the clusters is the following:

Cluster 1: Contains firms whose criteria- variables have a medium frequency of 2.44 and a standard deviation of 0.623.
Cluster 2: Contains firms whose criteria- variables have a medium frequency of 3.522 and a standard deviation of 0.97.

Figure 36. Medium scores per cluster
(Source: SPSS data processing)

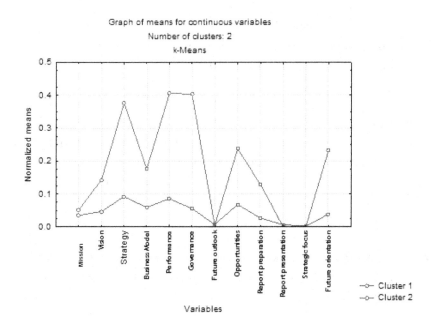

The cluster analysis shows that certain companies have reporting patters that increase the disclosure level for IR, while other organizations follow reporting habits that do not encourage too much this type of disclosure.

Therefore, this study offers the possibility to group companies according to the variables/ indicators included in the research. We conclude that these elements/ items are relevant for determining if a company has a certain degree of IR disclosure level.

This investigation aims to create a framework of disclosure elements/ items so that their medium scores define the group in which the company can be included with the corresponding reporting pattern for IR. Finally, we managed to find patterns that guide companies in setting their reporting attitude. The 10 IR disclosure items become the proper criteria for measuring IR disclosure levels. From a time perspective, we observed the significant changes from one year to another in the level of IR information presented in annual reports.

Results SPSS Part 2: Studying the Impact of External/ Internal Factors Upon the IR Disclosure Index

This part of the research studies the impacts of external and internal factors (as organizational characteristics and country- level indicators). The data contains the aggregated disclosure index on integrated reporting[5] and the assumed determinants/ impact factors:

The variables were coded as shown in Table 54.

In the first stage of the analysis, we performed statistical computations for determining the behavior of the impact factors (Figure 14). This step is marked by three stages, namely: overall, between, and within. The overall category refers to those statistics calculations that are based the total number of observations (2.425)[6]. The level of between includes those statistical computations that considered the 485 corporations (our sample of companies that had available data) independently of the time period. The within category holds the statistical calculations made according to specific time periods, but independently from the 485 companies. In this sense, we observe that the standard deviation differs from 0, so there are differences between the time frames.

We continued the analysis by applying the Hausman test. This is an essential check for deciding whether to choose the panel method with fixed effects or the one with random effects. The null hypothesis assumes that

Table 53. Descriptive statistics- relevant data

Variable	Obs	Mean	Std. Dev.	Min	Max
Ridi	2425	252.6078	374.9666	0	4463
pricepersh~e	2425	33.27012	97.69643	0	2741.68
marketvalue	2425	20261.4	42071.68	0	592479.3
accounting~s	2425	2.018557	1.704702	0	4
noofemploy~s	2425	49257.62	77990.76	0	611020
operatingi~e	2425	2576057	5585934	-6029118	5.52e+07
totalasset~a	2425	8.51e+07	3.10e+08	0	3.09e+09
debttoequity	2425	126.048	3245.713	-46633.33	96050
marketcapi~n	2425	73.41671	48.07732	0	248.02
Gdp	2425	43400.65	15699.53	0	113738.7
Hdi	2425	3.686132	12.64084	0	146
Cpi	2425	32.32701	31.95879	0	91

(Source: SPSS data processing)

Table 54.

the aggregated disclosure index on IR- Ridi price per share - pricepersh~e market value – marketvalue accounting standards - accounting~s number of employees - noofemploy~s operating income- operatingi~e	total assets - totalasset~a debt to equity - debttoequity market capitalization - marketcapi~n gross domestic product – gdp human development index – hdi corruption perception index - cpi

the unique errors are not correlated with the regression. The Hausman test is based on the idea that the estimator of the additional effects is affected if the individual effects are correlated with the explanatory variables while the fixed effects estimator remains the same (as being fixed by nature) but becomes less efficient when this correlation does not exist.

After applying the test, we decided that our model has two types of factors:

1. Time evolving factors
2. Factors that do not change with time passing

Table 55 shows the statistical results obtained in both cases:

The factors/ determinants for which we obtained significant differences are: number of employees, total assets, market capitalization, GDP, HDI, accounting standard, industry, legal system.

Figure 37. Descriptive statistics on three levels: overall, between and within
(Source: SPSS data processing)

Variable		Mean	Std. Dev.	Min	Max	Observations	
ridi	overall	252.6078	374.9666	0	4463	N =	2425
	between		310.0348	1.6	3077	n =	485
	within		211.2747	-1615.992	2690.608	T =	5
pricep~e	overall	33.27012	97.69643	0	2741.68	N =	2425
	between		92.23855	0	1894.132	n =	485
	within		32.41422	-832.8619	880.8181	T =	5
market~e	overall	20261.4	42071.68	0	592479.3	N =	2425
	between		40546.5	0	374565.7	n =	485
	within		11345.51	-199143.5	287849.7	T =	5
accoun~s	overall	2.018557	1.704702	0	4	N =	2425
	between		1.70611	0	4	n =	485
	within		0	2.018557	2.018557	T =	5
noofem~s	overall	49257.62	77990.76	0	611020	N =	2425
	between		76460.13	0	547422.8	n =	485
	within		15686.13	-379666.4	203323.6	T =	5
operat~e	overall	2576057	5585934	-6029118	5.52e+07	N =	2425
	between		5318207	-782000	4.22e+07	n =	485
	within		1722209	-1.97e+07	2.41e+07	T =	5
totala~a	overall	8.51e+07	3.10e+08	0	3.09e+09	N =	2425
	between		3.08e+08	0	2.61e+09	n =	485
	within		3.01e+07	-3.81e+08	7.09e+08	T =	5
debtto~y	overall	126.048	3245.713	-46633.33	96050	N =	2425
	between		766.6844	-5403.962	8646.52	n =	485
	within		3154.016	-55153.8	87529.53	T =	5
market~n	overall	73.41671	48.07732	0	248.02	N =	2425
	between		26.73708	0	142.324	n =	485
	within		39.9717	-68.90729	179.1127	T =	5
gdp	overall	43400.65	15699.53	0	113738.7	N =	2425
	between		15487.85	0	106809	n =	485
	within		2645.297	27778.87	52601.43	T =	5
hdi	overall	3.686132	12.64084	0	146	N =	2425
	between		5.026381	0	29.628	n =	485
	within		11.60035	-25.41187	120.0581	T =	5
cpi	overall	32.32701	31.95879	0	91	N =	2425
	between		5.6316	.94	41.8	n =	485
	within		31.45952	-.1729895	81.52701	T =	5

The panel models have a major role in preparing cross- sectional and transversal analysis being a coherent measurement of data even from a perspective of unobserved factors. The regressions that interfere in the panel model are different from other regression types because of the double index on its variables, and the equation becomes:

$$Y_{it} = \alpha_i + X_{it} \times \beta + u_{it}, i = 1,\dots,N; t = 1,\dots,T \qquad (1)$$

where *i* represents the studied entities and *t* means time period.

Panel data are models with fixed effects or additional effects. In the fixed effects modes, the error component αi can be correlated with regression factors $X_{it,}$ the research hypothesis being that there is no correlation between

Table 55. Statistical results based on Hausman test

ridi	Coef.	Std. Err.	z	P > z	[95% Conf.	Interval]
Tvexogenous: Time Evolving						
pricepersh~e	-.012443	.1002643	-0.12	0.901	-.2089573	.1840713
marketvalue	.0001866	.0004196	0.44	0.657	-.0006358	.001009
noofemploy~s	-.0002898	.0001595	-1.82	0.03	-.0006024	.0000228
operatingi~e	-4.05e-07	3.04e-06	-0.13	0.894	-6.37e-06	5.56e-06
totalasset~a	4.60e-07	4.33e-08	10.62	0.000	3.75e-07	5.45e-07
debttoequity	.0008368	.0014915	0.56	0.575	-.0020864	.00376
marketcapi~n	.8597423	.1585408	5.42	0.000	.549008	1.170477
gdp	.0017845	.0009413	1.90	0.02	-.0000604	.0036294
hdi	-1.179751	.4478155	-2.63	0.008	-2.057453	-.3020487
cpi	-.1526577	.2902581	-0.53	0.599	-.721553	.4162377
TIexogenous: Do Not Change With Time						
accounting~s	-19.14448	7.727559	-2.48	0.013	-34.29022	-3.998745
industry	5.33483	2.274068	2.35	0.019	.877738	9.791922
country	2.543054	2.288969	1.11	0.267	-1.943242	7.029351
legalsystem	69.02139	28.4521	2.43	0.015	13.25631	124.7865

Note. TV refers to time varying; TI refers to time invariant.
(Source: SPSS data processing)

regression factors and the additional component of the error e_{it}. The additional effects models assume that α_i error is additional, while the error is not correlated with the regression factors (Baum, 2001). The panel analysis starts by determining the type of regression suitable for the study, more specific if we should involve a normal regression or a panel one. In order to find the best solution, we need to check if there are any individual effects (fixed model). In the fixed model effect (Aparaschivei, 2011), the most often met estimator is 'within'. This implies using the OLS- least square method. In this analysis, we obtain the model through estimating the individual mean values, thus eliminating the fixed effects (those variables that do not change with time). The models with additional effects, term α_i are incorporated in the error term, and are assumed not to be correlated with the explanatory variables during each period of time. This model implies running tests for heteroscedasticity. The next stage involved the application of Wald test (F = 89.46, p = 0.000) whose null hypothesis states that there is autocorrelation of first degree.

From the statistical computations on defining the factors' behavior for the 2425 observations we deduct that the standard deviation is 0, so there are differences/ changes between the studied time intervals, as well as the fact that the database is in a sort of equilibrium.

Further on, we applied the following model:

$$Y = b_0 + X_1 + X_2 + X_3 + X_4 + X_5 + X_6 + X_7 + X_8 + X_9 + X_{10} + X_{11} + X_{12} + X_{13} + X_{14} + e \qquad (2)$$

where:

$Y = di$; $b_0 =$ constant variable;
$X_1 =$ price per share;
$X_2 =$ market value;
$X_3 =$ accounting standards;
$X_4 =$ no. of employees;
$X_5 =$ total assets (TA);
$X_6 =$ operating income;
$X_7 =$ debt to equity;
$X_8 =$ industry;
$X_9 =$ country;
$X_{10} =$ legal system;
$X_{11} =$ market capitalization;
$X_{12} =$ GDP;
$X_{13} =$ HDI;
$X_{14} =$ CPI;
$e =$ standard errors

Table 56 shows the results for the regression model stated above.

The null hypothesis states that all the coefficients of the independent variables differ from 0, which is true also for the current case, so we can deduct that the independent variables have an effect on the dependent one. The obtained results are explained by the fact that for some of the companies considered in the research, the dependent variable can be associated with the independent ones: number of employees, total assets, market capitalization, GDP, HDI, accounting standard, industry, legal system. In addition, for these companies, the relation between variables will last in time.

Table 56. Results for the regression model

ridi	Coef.	Std. Err.	z	P>|z|	[95% Conf.	Interval]
pricepersh~e	-.0070234	.0984923	-0.07	0.943	-.2000647	.1860179
marketvalue	.0001995	.0004157	0.48	0.631	-.0006153	.0010143
accounting~s	-19.07808	7.504614	-2.54	0.011	-33.78685	-4.369306
noofemploy~s	-.0003018	.0001564	-1.93	0.04	-.0006085	4.81e-06
totalasset~a	4.60e-07	4.22e-08	10.90	0.000	3.77e-07	5.42e-07
operatingi~e	-1.61e-07	3.02e-06	-0.05	0.957	-6.09e-06	5.77e-06
debttoequity	.0008796	.0015015	0.59	0.558	-.0020633	.0038225
industry	5.298346	2.2093	2.40	0.016	.9681989	.628494
country	2.819922	.213562	1.27	0.203	-1.518582	7.158421
legalsystem	67.67813	27.61297	2.45	0.014	13.5577	121.7986
marketcapi~n	.7969142	.1456822	5.47	0.000	.5113823	1.082446
gdp	.001983	.0009065	2.19	0.029	.0002062	.0037598
hdi	-1.065324	.4405745	-2.42	0.016	-1.928835	-.2018141
cpi	.0941972	.184839	0.51	0.610	-.2680807	.456475
_cons	-38.20658	69.62755	-0.55	0.583	-174.6741	98.2609
sigma_u	241.49709					
sigma_e	233.30457					
rho	.51724948 (fraction of variance du_i)					

(Source: SPSS data processing)

In order to test our model for additional effects, we included the Breusch-Pagan Lagrange (LM) multiplicative test. The null hypothesis of this test states that between companies the attitude towards the determinants/ factors is 0. This means that here should be no significant difference between companies' reporting behaviour (the disclosure of information specific for integrated reporting) and the organizational characteristics/ country- level indicators. In other words, there is no case when a certain factors maintains a higher impact on a company in the detriment of other, or that these variables intertwine.

$$ridi[id,t] = Xb + u[id] + e[id,t] \qquad (3)$$

Estimated results:

+	Var	$sd = sqrt\left(Var\right)$
ridi	140599.9	374.9666
e	55773.23	236.1636
u	84966.92	291.4909

$$Var\left(u\right) = 0$$
Test: $chi2\left(1\right) = 1764.42$
$$Prob > chi2 = 0.0000$$

According to the results of this test, we accept the null hypothesis that the attitude of corporations in terms of reporting behaviour towards impact factors/ determinants is the same in all cases.

Then we should apply the transversal testing, whose hypothesis states that the cross- sectional dimensions of this study are independent. For testing the hypothesis, we use the CD test. The results show the following values:

Pesaran's test of cross sectional independence = 6.452, p = 0.0000

Average absolute value of the off-diagonal elements = 0.425

Therefore, we reject the null hypothesis (p < 0.005), proving in the same time the existence of a cross- dependence between the studied dimensions. The medium correlation is 0.538.

The data considered in this study comply with the heteroscedasticity conditions (chi2 (14) = 86842.55; p > chi2 = 0.0000). Wooldridge test confirms the existence of serial correlations between the dependent and the independent variables (F = 13.522, p-value = 0.002).

Therefore, the level of disclosure index for integrated reporting is influenced only by certain factors included in the analysis, namely: number of employees, total assets, market capitalization, GDP, HDI, accounting standards, industry, and legal system. Companies' reporting attitude towards the factors/ determinants is the same, so that we have strong arguments to sustain that IR disclosure level is affected by the correlation/ connection with the independents variables (factors of impact). The explanation from an economic perspective would be that the higher a company is (organizational size in terms of number of employees and total assets), the most probably that will be interested in reporting more extra- financial information in addition to the financial one, and having an IR approach. As socially responsible investors become aware of the non-financial information impact on decision-making and corporations' performance, looking beyond the financial side of business, we are not surprised that market capitalization influences IR disclosure. Then, for sure the degree of economic development of a country (measured by its GDP) would impact the ability and attitude of corporations for applying IR. In addition, the cultural factor of HDI also suggests a certain reporting behavior oriented towards non-financial information, besides the financial one. The legal system will impact IR disclosure as countries can have stakeholder-oriented policies versus shareholder oriented ones. Industry is a relevant factor for the disclosure on IR as certain industries would present more IR information than others (e.g. companies from environmental sectors versus banking sector). Finally, accounting standards represent the main authority in the corporate reporting field, and therefore the position of an organization towards accounting policies and standard would impact the structure of the annual report and the degree of IR information.

ENDNOTES

[1]   We analyzed only 10 items from the DI because of time constraints and paper dimension limitations (there would not have been sufficient time to analyze in details all the items/ elements from our DI scale from a statistical perspective, and then it would be impossible to allocate too much to this chapter because of thesis dimension limitations). Then, these 10 items are considered the most important because they are also part of the IIRC framework.

[2]   Just to add that Chi-square was applied for all the 10 mentioned element from the IR disclosure index.

[3]   The statistical results obtained for the five years are: Chi-Square = 254.87817, df = 3 (adjusted), p = 0.000 for 2009; Chi-Square = 214.525, df = 3 (adjusted), p = 0.000 for 2010; Chi-Square = 118.807, df = 3 (adjusted), p = 0.000 for 2011; Chi-Square = 100.08, df = 3 (adjusted) , p = 0.000 for 2012; Chi-Square = 337.384, df = 3 (adjusted) , p = 0.000 for 2013.

4   The results per year are: Chi-Square = 146.942, p = 0.000 (2009); Chi-Square = 597.425, p = 0.000 (2010); Chi-Square = 427.982, p = 0.000 (2011); Chi-Square = 4.763, p = 0.029 (2012); Chi-Square = 211.926, p = 0.000 (2013).

5   This is expressed as the sum of disclosure frequencies of all the elements included in the IR integration scale.

6   The total number of observations represents the total numbers of annual reports considered in the study for all the five years period and that were available on the companies' websites or published on various sites.

Conclusion

The current work develops a disclosure index for measuring the level or IR. This 'integration scale' (that also stands for an original *prototype framework*) was built starting from IIRC framework and the comments received from international organizations and members of accountancy profession. The main purpose was to find the main IR determinants from an international perspective. We have tested the prototype framework on 600 corporations, models of best corporate citizenship. Data gathering was done using Tropes semantic software, while data analysis and interpretation involved SPSS computation and testing. Only 485 companies from the total sample had available reports in all the years of analysis. Therefore, we continued with the statistical study for these corporations, still including more than 2.000 observations (annual reports from our sample in all the five years). After applying several tests in SPSS, we found that IR registers significant evolutions in time- from a year to another. Another conclusion was that the diversity of companies generated different reporting behaviors, as we obtained significant discrepancies in the level of DI, with some exceptions in which the degree of IR was similar between companies in a certain year. Regarding the final stage of the research, we identified the following factors with a relevant statistical impact on the disclosure of IR information: number of employees, total assets, market capitalization, industry (as organizational characteristics, accounting standards), GDP, HDI, legal system (as country- level indicators).

In the construction of our model of integrated reporting framework, we considered the results obtained in our first study: the survey on IR addressed to accountancy profession. The questions from the survey were meant to draw an image upon what companies should include in their integrated reports, and how this type of reporting could be organized from the perspective of accountancy profession- a relevant authority in the corporate reporting area.

Further research can be conducted in the field of integrated corporate reporting, by testing our model on a larger sample, with the possibility of grouping the countries into regions and analyzing the results from a geographical perspective, and even geo-political implications. Nevertheless, our model can still be improved, by adding more variables or changing the measurements criteria in the disclosure index.

Appendix

APPENDIX 1: SAMPLE FOR TESTING THE IR LEVEL IN THE ANNUAL REPORTS

Table 1.

Crt. No.	Organization	Accounting Standards	Industry	Country
1	ABB	US standards (GAAP)	Industrial Goods & Services	Switzerland
2	Abbott Laboratories	-	Health Care	United States
3	Abercrombie & Fitch	US standards (GAAP)	Retail	United States
4	ABM Industries	US standards (GAAP)	Industrial Goods & Services	United States
5	Accenture	US standards (GAAP)	Technology	Ireland
6	Accor	IFRS	Travel & Leisure	France
7	Activision Blizzard	-	Technology	United States
8	Adecco Group	US standards (GAAP)	Industrial Goods & Services	United Kingdom
9	Adidas	IFRS	Personal & Household Goods	Germany
10	Adobe Systems	US standards (GAAP)	Technology	United States
11	Advanced Micro Devices	US standards (GAAP)	Technology	United States
12	Aflac	US standards (GAAP)	Insurance	United States
13	Agilent Technologies	US standards (GAAP)	Health Care	United States
14	Airgas	US standards (GAAP)	Retail	United States
15	Ajinomoto	-	Food & Beverage	Japan
16	Akzo Nobel	IFRS	Chemicals	Netherlands

Table 1. Continued

Crt. No.	Organization	Accounting Standards	Industry	Country
17	Alcatel-Lucent	-	Telecommunications	France
18	Alcoa	US standards (GAAP)	Basic Resources	United States
19	All Nippon Airways	US standards (GAAP)	Travel & Leisure	Japan
20	Alliance Data Systems	US standards (GAAP)	Financial Services	United States
21	Alliance One International	US standards (GAAP)	Personal & Household Goods	United States
22	Allianz	IFRS	Insurance	Germany
23	Allstate	US standards (GAAP)	Insurance	United States
24	Alstom	IFRS	Industrial Goods & Services	France
25	American Eagle Outfitters	-	Retail	United States
26	Amerigroup	US standards (GAAP)	Health Care	United States
27	AmerisourceBergen	-	Retail	United States
28	Amgen	US standards (GAAP)	Health Care	United States
29	Anixter International	US standards (GAAP)	Retail	United States
30	AOL	US standards (GAAP)	Technology	United States
31	Apple	US standards (GAAP)	Technology	United States
32	Applied Materials	US standards (GAAP)	Technology	United States
33	Arrow Electronics	US standards (GAAP)	Retail	United States
34	Assicurazioni Generali	-	Insurance	Italy
35	Association of Chartered Certified Accountants ACCA	-	Other	United Kingdom
36	AstraZeneca	IFRS	Health Care	United Kingdom
37	AT&T	US standards (GAAP)	Telecommunications	United States
38	Autodesk	US standards (GAAP)	Technology	United States
39	Automatic Data Processing	US standards (GAAP)	Financial Services	United States

continued on following page

Table 1. Continued

Crt. No.	Organization	Accounting Standards	Industry	Country
40	Aviva	IFRS	Insurance	United Kingdom
41	Avnet	US standards (GAAP)	Retail	United States
42	Avon Products	US standards (GAAP)	Personal & Household Goods	United States
43	AXA	IFRS	Insurance	France
44	BAE Systems	-	Industrial Goods & Services	Australia
45	BANK OF AMERICA	US standards (GAAP)	Banks	United States
46	Bank of New York Mellon	-	Banks	United States
47	Barclays	IFRS	Banks	United Kingdom
48	BASF	IFRS	Chemicals	Germany
49	Bayer	IFRS	Chemicals	Germany
50	BB&T Corp	US standards (GAAP)	Banks	United States
51	Becton Dickinson	-	Health Care	United States
52	Beiersdorf	IFRS	Personal & Household Goods	Germany
53	Bemis	-	Industrial Goods & Services	United States
54	BERKSHIRE HATHAWAY	-	Insurance	United States
55	Best Buy	-	Retail	United States
56	BG Group	IFRS	Basic Resources	United Kingdom
57	BHP Billiton	IFRS	Basic Resources	Australia
58	BMW	-	Automobiles & Parts	Germany
59	BNP Paribas	IFRS	Banks	France
60	Boeing	US standards (GAAP)	Industrial Goods & Services	United States
61	Bombardier	Local standards	Industrial Goods & Services	Canada
62	Boston Scientific	-	Health Care	United States
63	Bouygues	IFRS	Construction & Materials	France
64	BP	IFRS	Oil & Gas	United Kingdom

continued on following page

Table 1. Continued

Crt. No.	Organization	Accounting Standards	Industry	Country
65	Brightpoint	US standards (GAAP)	Media	United States
66	Brinker International	US standards (GAAP)	Food & Beverage	United States
67	British Airways	IFRS	Travel & Leisure	United Kingdom
68	British American Tobacco	IFRS	Personal & Household Goods	United Kingdom
69	Broadcom	US standards (GAAP)	Technology	United States
70	Broadridge Financial Solutions	US standards (GAAP)	Financial Services	United States
71	BT Group	IFRS	Telecommunications	United Kingdom
72	Bunge	US standards (GAAP)	Food & Beverage	United States
73	C.H. Robinson Worldwide	US standards (GAAP)	Industrial Goods & Services	United States
74	CACI International	US standards (GAAP)	Technology	United States
75	Caesars Entertainment	US standards (GAAP)	Travel & Leisure	United States
76	Canon	US standards (GAAP)	Technology	Japan
77	Capital One Financial	US standards (GAAP)	Financial Services	United States
78	Cardinal Health	-	Retail	United States
79	Carlsberg	IFRS	Food & Beverage	Denmark
80	Caterpillar	US standards (GAAP)	Industrial Goods & Services	United States
81	Cathay Life Insurance	NA	Insurance	China
82	Cathay Pacific Airways	-	Travel & Leisure	China
83	CB Richard Ellis Group	NA	Real Estate	United States
84	Celestica	Local standards	Technology	Canada
85	Charles Schwab	US standards (GAAP)	Financial Services	United States
86	Cheesecake Factory	-	Food & Beverage	United States
87	Chevron	US standards (GAAP)	Oil & Gas	United States

continued on following page

Table 1. Continued

Crt. No.	Organization	Accounting Standards	Industry	Country
88	CHINA MOBILE	IFRS	Telecommunications	China
89	China Mobile Communications	IFRS	Telecommunications	China
90	CHINA PETROLEUM	-	Oil & Gas	China
91	China Railway Construction	IFRS	Industrial Goods & Services	China
92	Cie Financière Richemont	IFRS	Personal & Household Goods	France
93	Cigna	US standards (GAAP)	Health Care	United States
94	Cintas	US standards (GAAP)	Industrial Goods & Services	United States
95	Cisco Systems	-	Technology	United States
96	Citigroup	US standards (GAAP)	Banks	United States
97	Cliffs Natural Resources	US standards (GAAP)	Construction & Materials	United States
98	Clorox	US standards (GAAP)	Personal & Household Goods	United States
99	CLP Holdings Limited	Local standards	Utilities	China
100	CNP Assurances	-	Insurance	France
101	Coach	US standards (GAAP)	Personal & Household Goods	United States
102	Coca-Cola	Local standards with some IASC guidelines	Food & Beverage	United States
103	Coca-Cola Içecek AS	Local standards with some IASC guidelines	Food & Beverage	Turkey
104	Cognizant Technology Solutions	US standards (GAAP)	Technology	United States
105	Colgate-Palmolive	US standards (GAAP)	Personal & Household Goods	United States
106	Collective Brands	NA	Retail	United States
107	Comcast	US standards (GAAP)	Telecommunications	United States
108	Commonwealth Bank of Australia	-	Banks	Australia
109	CommScope	US standards (GAAP)	Technology	United States

continued on following page

Table 1. Continued

Crt. No.	Organization	Accounting Standards	Industry	Country
110	Community Health Systems	-	Health Care	United States
111	Compagnie de Saint-Gobain	-	Construction & Materials	France
112	Compal Electronics	Local standards	Technology	Taiwan
113	Corning	US standards (GAAP)	Technology	United States
114	Costco Wholesale	-	Retail	United States
115	CPFL Energia	Local standards	Utilities	Brazil
116	CPN	Local standards	Utilities	France
117	Cracker Barrel Old Country Store	US standards (GAAP)	Food & Beverage	United States
118	Credit Suisse	US standards (GAAP)	Banks	Switzerland
119	Crown Holdings	US standards (GAAP)	Industrial Goods & Services	United States
120	CSX Corp.	US standards (GAAP)	Industrial Goods & Services	United States
121	Cummins Inc.	US standards (GAAP)	Industrial Goods & Services	United States
122	CVS Caremark Corp.	US standards (GAAP)	Health Care	United States
123	D.R. Horton	-	Construction & Materials	United States
124	Daimler	IFRS	Automobiles & Parts	Germany
125	Danaher	US standards (GAAP)	Health Care	United States
126	Danone GmbH	IFRS	Food & Beverage	Germany
127	Darden Restaurants, Inc.	US standards (GAAP)	Travel & Leisure	United States
128	DaVita	US standards (GAAP)	Health Care	United States
129	Dean Foods	US standards (GAAP)	Food & Beverage	United States
130	Deere	-	Automobiles & Parts	United States
131	Delta Air Lines	-	Travel & Leisure	United States
132	Delta Lloyd Group	-	Insurance	Netherlands
133	DEMOS	Local standards	Other	United Kingdom

continued on following page

Table 1. Continued

Crt. No.	Organization	Accounting Standards	Industry	Country
134	Denso	Local standards	Automobiles & Parts	Japan
135	Deutsche Bank	IFRS	Banks	Germany
136	Deutsche Lufthansa AG	IFRS	Travel & Leisure	Germany
137	Deutsche Post (DHL)	IFRS	Industrial Goods & Services	Germany
138	Devon Energy	US standards (GAAP)	Basic Resources	United States
139	Diageo	-	Food & Beverage	United Kingdom
140	Diesel & Motor Engineering PLC	Local standards	Construction & Materials	Sri Lanka
141	Discover Financial Services	US standards (GAAP)	Financial Services	United States
142	Discovery Communications	US standards (GAAP)	Media	United States
143	DnB NOR	IFRS	Financial Services	Norway
144	DNV Business Assurance	-	Financial Services	Norway
145	Dollar General	US standards (GAAP)	Retail	United States
146	Domtar	US standards (GAAP)	Basic Resources	United States
147	Dongfeng Motor	Local standards	Automobiles & Parts	China
148	Doosan Infracore Co Ltd	Local standards	Construction & Materials	South Korea
149	DTE Energy	US standards (GAAP)	Telecommunications	United States
150	Dun & Bradstreet	US standards (GAAP)	Financial Services	United States
151	E*Trade Financial	-	Financial Services	United States
152	E.ON	IFRS	Utilities	Germany
153	EADS	-	Industrial Goods & Services	Netherlands
154	EAPB - European Association of Public Banks	-	Other	Belgium
155	Eastman Kodak	-	Health Care	United States
156	Eaton	US standards (GAAP)	Industrial Goods & Services	United States

continued on following page

Table 1. Continued

Crt. No.	Organization	Accounting Standards	Industry	Country
157	EBAY	US standards (GAAP)	Retail	United States
158	ECB European Central Bank	-	Banks	Germany
159	Ecopetrol S.A	Local standards	Oil & Gas	Colombia
160	Eden International	-	Other	Cote D'ivoire
161	EDF Energy	IFRS	Utilities	United Kingdom
162	Edison	US standards (GAAP)	Utilities	Italy
163	Edison International	US standards (GAAP)	Utilities	United States
164	EFFAS	IFRS	Other	Germany
165	Eiffage	IFRS	Construction & Materials	France
166	Electrolux	IFRS	Personal & Household Goods	Sweden
167	Electronic Arts	-	Technology	United States
168	Eletrobrás	US standards (GAAP)	Utilities	Brazil
169	Eli Lilly	-	Health Care	United States
170	EMC	US standards (GAAP)	Technology	United States
171	EMCOR Group	-	Construction & Materials	United States
172	Emerson Electric	US standards (GAAP)	Personal & Household Goods	United States
173	ENAGAS S.A	IFRS	Oil & Gas	Spain
174	EnBW Energie Baden-Württemberg AG	IFRS	Utilities	Germany
175	EnCana	Local standards	Oil & Gas	Canada
176	Endesa	IFRS	Utilities	Spain
177	Enel S.p.A.	IFRS	Utilities	Italy
178	Energizer Holdings	IFRS	Personal & Household Goods	United States
179	Engro Chemical Pakistan Limited	Local standards	Chemicals	Pakistan
180	ENI	IFRS	Oil & Gas	United States
181	Equifax	US standards (GAAP)	Financial Services	United States

continued on following page

Table 1. Continued

Crt. No.	Organization	Accounting Standards	Industry	Country
182	Equity Residential	US standards (GAAP)	Real Estate	United States
183	Ernst & Young	-	Financial Services	United Kingdom
184	Estée Lauder	US standards (GAAP)	Personal & Household Goods	United States
185	EUROBANK Group of Companies	IFRS	Banks	Greece
186	European Association of Co- operative Banks - EACB	-	Other	Belgium
187	European Investment Bank	-	Banks	Luxembourg
188	Evonik Industries	IFRS	Chemicals	Germany
189	Exelon	US standards (GAAP)	Utilities	United States
190	Expedia	-	Technology	United States
191	Expeditors International of Washington	US standards (GAAP)	Industrial Goods & Services	United States
192	Express Scripts	US standards (GAAP)	Health Care	United States
193	EXXON MOBIL	US standards (GAAP)	Oil & Gas	United States
194	Family Dollar Stores	-	Retail	United States
195	FBE European Banking Federation	-	Other	Belgium
196	FedEx	US standards (GAAP)	Industrial Goods & Services	United States
197	Ferrovial	-	Construction & Materials	Spain
198	Fiat	IFRS	Automobiles & Parts	Italy
199	Fibria Celulose S.A	Local standards	Basic Resources	Brazil
200	Fidelity Investments	-	Financial Services	United Kingdom
201	Fidelity National Information Services	US standards (GAAP)	Financial Services	United States
202	Fifth Third Bancorp	-	Banks	United States
203	Finmeccanica	IFRS	Industrial Goods & Services	Italy
204	First Data	NA	Financial Services	United States
205	FirstEnergy	US standards (GAAP)	Utilities	United States

continued on following page

Table 1. Continued

Crt. No.	Organization	Accounting Standards	Industry	Country
206	Fiserv	US standards (GAAP)	Financial Services	United States
207	Flextronics International	US standards (GAAP)	Technology	Singapore
208	Fluor	US standards (GAAP)	Construction & Materials	United States
209	Fomento de Construcciones	IFRS	Construction & Materials	Spain
210	Foot Locker	-	Retail	United States
211	Ford Motor	US standards (GAAP)	Automobiles & Parts	United States
212	FOURLIS Group of Companies	IFRS	Personal & Household Goods	Greece
213	France Télécom	US standards (GAAP)	Telecommunications	France
214	Franklin Resources	-	Financial Services	United States
215	Franz Haniel	-	Retail	Germany
216	Fraport AG	IFRS	Travel & Leisure	Germany
217	Freeport-McMoRan Copper & Gold	US standards (GAAP)	Oil & Gas	United States
218	Fresenius	-	Health Care	Germany
219	Fujitsu	Local standards	Technology	Japan
220	Fuller, Smith & turner plc	IFRS	Food & Beverage	United Kingdom
221	Gap	US standards (GAAP)	Retail	United States
222	GOOGLE	US standards (GAAP)	Technology	United States
223	Graphic Packaging Holding	US standards (GAAP)	Industrial Goods & Services	United States
224	Graybar Electric	US standards (GAAP)	Retail	United States
225	Gruppo Banca Carige	-	Banks	Italy
226	Guess	-	Personal & Household Goods	United States
227	H.J. Heinz	-	Food & Beverage	United States
228	HALCOR Group of Companies	IFRS	Basic Resources	Greece
229	Hammerson	IFRS	Real Estate	United Kingdom

continued on following page

Table 1. Continued

Crt. No.	Organization	Accounting Standards	Industry	Country
230	Hanesbrands	-	Personal & Household Goods	United States
231	Harris	US standards (GAAP)	Technology	United States
232	Hartford Financial Services	US standards (GAAP)	Insurance	United States
233	Hasbro, Inc.	US standards (GAAP)	Personal & Household Goods	United States
234	Health Management Associates	US standards (GAAP)	Health Care	United States
235	Health Net	US standards (GAAP)	Health Care	United States
236	HeidelbergCement AG	Local standards	Construction & Materials	Germany
237	Heineken	IFRS	Food & Beverage	Netherlands
238	Henkel	-	Personal & Household Goods	Germany
239	Henry Schein	-	Retail	United States
240	Heraeus Holding	IFRS	Basic Resources	Germany
241	Herman Miller	US standards (GAAP)	Personal & Household Goods	United States
242	Hewlett-Packard Co.	US standards (GAAP)	Technology	United States
243	Hines Colin	-	Real Estate	United Kingdom
244	Hitachi	-	Personal & Household Goods	Japan
245	HNI	US standards (GAAP)	Personal & Household Goods	United States
246	Hochtief	-	Construction & Materials	Germany
247	Home Depot	-	Retail	United States
248	Honda Motor	-	Automobiles & Parts	Japan
249	Honeywell International	US standards (GAAP)	Industrial Goods & Services	United States
250	Hoosier Energy Rural Electric Coop	NA	Utilities	United States
251	Hormel Foods Corp.	US standards (GAAP)	Food & Beverage	United States
252	Host Hotels & Resorts	-	Travel & Leisure	United States
253	HSBC Holdings plc	IFRS	Banks	United Kingdom

continued on following page

Table 1. Continued

Crt. No.	Organization	Accounting Standards	Industry	Country
254	Huawei Technologies	Local standards	Technology	China
255	HudBay Minerals Inc	Local standards	Basic Resources	Canada
256	Humana	US standards (GAAP)	Health Care	United States
257	Hundred Group of Finance	-	Financial Services	United Kingdom
258	Husky Energy	Local standards	Basic Resources	Canada
259	Hyatt Hotels	US standards (GAAP)	Travel & Leisure	United States
260	Hynix Semiconductor	Local standards	Technology	South Korea
261	Hyundai Heavy Industries	-	Industrial Goods & Services	South Korea
262	Hyundai Motor	Local standards	Automobiles & Parts	South Korea
263	IBM	-	Technology	United States
264	ICAEW	-	Other	United Kingdom
265	ICAS	-	Other	United Kingdom
266	Illinois Tool Works	-	Industrial Goods & Services	United States
267	Imerys	-	Technology	France
268	Imperial Tobacco	IFRS	Personal & Household Goods	United Kingdom
269	IND & COMM BK	-	Banks	China
270	INDITEX	-	Personal & Household Goods	Spain
271	Indra	IFRS	Financial Services	Spain
272	Infineon Technologies	-	Technology	Germany
273	Infosys Limited	Local standards	Technology	India
274	ING Groep NV	IFRS	Banks	Netherlands
275	Ingram Micro	US standards (GAAP)	Retail	United States
276	Inmet Mining	Local standards	Basic Resources	Canada

continued on following page

Table 1. Continued

Crt. No.	Organization	Accounting Standards	Industry	Country
277	Insight Enterprises	US standards (GAAP)	Retail	United States
278	Intel	-	Technology	United States
279	Intermon Oxfam	-	Other	Spain
280	International Flavors & Fragrances Inc	-	Personal & Household Goods	United States
281	International Paper	-	Basic Resources	United States
282	Interserve Plc	US standards (GAAP)	Industrial Goods & Services	United Kingdom
283	Intuit	US standards (GAAP)	Technology	United States
284	Iron Mountain	US standards (GAAP)	Industrial Goods & Services	United States
285	ISAGEN S.A. « ESP »	Local standards	Utilities	Colombia
286	ITC Ltd	Local standards	Travel & Leisure	India
287	ITT	US standards (GAAP)	Industrial Goods & Services	United States
288	J.B. Hunt Transport Services	US standards (GAAP)	Industrial Goods & Services	United States
289	J.C. Penney	US standards (GAAP)	Retail	United States
290	J.P. Morgan Chase	US standards (GAAP)	Banks	United States
291	Jabil Circuit	US standards (GAAP)	Technology	United States
292	Jacobs Engineering Group	US standards (GAAP)	Construction & Materials	United States
293	Japan Post Holdings	Local standards	Industrial Goods & Services	Japan
294	Japan Tobacco	Local standards	Personal & Household Goods	Japan
295	Jarden	US standards (GAAP)	Personal & Household Goods	United States
296	JFE Holdings	Local standards	Basic Resources	Japan
297	Johnson & Johnson	-	Health Care	United States
298	Johnson Controls	-	Automobiles & Parts	United States

continued on following page

Table 1. Continued

Crt. No.	Organization	Accounting Standards	Industry	Country
299	Jones Group	US standards (GAAP)	Personal & Household Goods	United States
300	Jones Lang LaSalle	-	Real Estate	United States
301	Juniper Networks	US standards (GAAP)	Technology	United States
302	Kajima	Local standards	Construction & Materials	Japan
303	Kao	Local standards	Personal & Household Goods	Japan
304	Kawasaki Heavy Industries	Local standards	Industrial Goods & Services	Japan
305	KB Home	-	Construction & Materials	United States
306	KDDI	Local standards	Telecommunications	Japan
307	Kelly Services	US standards (GAAP)	Industrial Goods & Services	United States
308	Keppel Land Limited	Local standards	Construction & Materials	Singapore
309	Kimberly-Clark Corp.	US standards (GAAP)	Personal & Household Goods	United States
310	Kindred Healthcare	-	Health Care	United States
311	Kirin Holdings	Local standards	Food & Beverage	Japan
312	Kirloskar Brothers Limited	Local standards	Industrial Goods & Services	India
313	Kobe Steel	-	Basic Resources	Japan
314	Koç Holding	Local standards with some IASC guidelines	Utilities	Turkey
315	Komatsu	US standards (GAAP)	Industrial Goods & Services	Japan
316	Owens-Illinois	US standards (GAAP)	Industrial Goods & Services	United States
317	Pacer International	US standards (GAAP)	Industrial Goods & Services	United States
318	Panasonic	US standards (GAAP)	Personal & Household Goods	Japan
319	Pernod Ricard	IFRS	Food & Beverage	France
320	PETROBRAS	Local standards	Oil & Gas	Brazil

continued on following page

Table 1. Continued

Crt. No.	Organization	Accounting Standards	Industry	Country
321	PETROCHINA	Local standards	Oil & Gas	China
322	Petronas	Local standards	Oil & Gas	Malaysia
323	Peugeot	IFRS	Automobiles & Parts	France
324	PharMerica	US standards (GAAP)	Health Care	United States
325	Pinnacle West Capital Corp.	US standards (GAAP)	Utilities	United States
326	Plains All American Pipeline	US standards (GAAP)	Oil & Gas	United States
327	PNC Financial Services Group	US standards (GAAP)	Banks	United States
328	Polo Ralph Lauren	-	Personal & Household Goods	United States
329	POSCO Engineering & Construction Co Ltd	Local standards	Basic Resources	South Korea
330	Poste Italiane	IFRS	Industrial Goods & Services	Italy
331	PPG Industries	US standards (GAAP)	Chemicals	United States
332	PPR	-	Personal & Household Goods	France
333	Priceline.com	US standards (GAAP)	Technology	United States
334	Pricewaterhouse Coopers	-	Financial Services	United Kingdom
335	PROCTER & GAMBLE	-	Personal & Household Goods	United States
336	Prudential plc	IFRS	Insurance	United Kingdom
337	PulteGroup	-	Construction & Materials	United States
338	Qantas Airways	IFRS	Travel & Leisure	Australia
339	Qualcomm	US standards (GAAP)	Telecommunications	United States
340	Quanta Computer	-	Technology	Taiwan
341	Quest Diagnostics	-	Health Care	United States
342	Randstad Holding	-	Industrial Goods & Services	Netherlands
343	Raymond James Financial	US standards (GAAP)	Financial Services	United States

continued on following page

Table 1. Continued

Crt. No.	Organization	Accounting Standards	Industry	Country
344	Raytheon	US standards (GAAP)	Industrial Goods & Services	United States
345	Realogy	US standards (GAAP)	Real Estate	United States
346	Reckitt Benckiser Group	-	Personal & Household Goods	United Kingdom
347	Regions Financial	US standards (GAAP)	Banks	United States
348	Reliance Steel & Aluminum	US standards (GAAP)	Retail	United States
349	Renault	IFRS	Automobiles & Parts	France
350	Repsol, S.A	IFRS	Oil & Gas	Spain
351	Research in Motion	-	Telecommunications	Canada
352	Reynolds American	-	Personal & Household Goods	United States
353	Ricoh	-	Technology	Japan
354	Rio Tinto	IFRS	Oil & Gas	United Kingdom
355	Robert Bosch	IFRS	Automobiles & Parts	Germany
356	Robert Half International	IFRS	Industrial Goods & Services	United States
357	RockTenn	US standards (GAAP)	Basic Resources	United States
358	Rockwell Automation Inc	US standards (GAAP)	Industrial Goods & Services	United States
359	Rosneft	-	Oil & Gas	Russia
360	Ross Stores	-	Retail	United States
361	ROYAL BANK OF CA	Local standards	Banks	Canada
362	Royal Bank of Scotland Group	Local standards	Banks	United Kingdom
363	Royal DSM NV	IFRS	Construction & Materials	Netherlands
364	Royal Dutch Shell	Local standards	Oil & Gas	Netherlands
365	Royal Mail Holdings	Local standards	Industrial Goods & Services	United Kingdom
366	Ruddick	-	Retail	United States
367	Ryder System	-	Industrial Goods & Services	United States

continued on following page

Table 1. Continued

Crt. No.	Organization	Accounting Standards	Industry	Country
368	SABIC	-	Chemicals	Saudi Arabia
369	SABMILLER	IFRS	Food & Beverage	United Kingdom
370	Samsung Engineering Co Ltd	Local standards	Construction & Materials	South Korea
371	Samsung Life Insurance	-	Insurance	South Korea
372	Sanmina-SCI	-	Technology	United States
373	ScanSource	-	Retail	United States
374	SCHLUMBERGER	US standards (GAAP)	Technology	Netherlands
375	Seaboard	US standards (GAAP)	Food & Beverage	United States
376	Seagate Technology	US standards (GAAP)	Technology	United States
377	Sealed Air	US standards (GAAP)	Industrial Goods & Services	United States
378	Sedex	Local standards	Other	United Kingdom
379	Sempra Energy	US standards (GAAP)	Utilities	United States
380	SFN Group	US standards (GAAP)	Industrial Goods & Services	United States
381	Shimizu	Local standards	Construction & Materials	Japan
382	Shinhan Financial Group Co Ltd	Local standards	Financial Services	South Korea
383	Shree Cement Limited	Local standards	Construction & Materials	India
384	Siemens AG	Local standards	Industrial Goods & Services	Germany
385	Sime Darby Berhad	Local standards	Industrial Goods & Services	Malaysia
386	Simon Property Group	-	Real Estate	United States
387	Singapore Airlines	-	Travel & Leisure	Singapore
388	Sinopec	IFRS	Oil & Gas	China
389	Sinosteel	Local standards	Basic Resources	China
390	SK Holdings	-	Oil & Gas	South Korea
391	Skanska	IFRS	Construction & Materials	Sweden

continued on following page

Table 1. Continued

Crt. No.	Organization	Accounting Standards	Industry	Country
392	Smithfield Foods	US standards (GAAP)	Food & Beverage	United States
393	Sodexo	-	Industrial Goods & Services	France
394	Softbank	Local standards	Telecommunications	Japan
395	Sompo Japan Insurance	Local standards	Insurance	Japan
396	Sonoco Products	-	Industrial Goods & Services	United States
397	Sony	US standards (GAAP)	Personal & Household Goods	Japan
398	Southern	US standards (GAAP)	Utilities	United States
399	Southwest Airlines	-	Travel & Leisure	United States
400	Spectrum Brands	US standards (GAAP)	Personal & Household Goods	United States
401	Sprint	US standards (GAAP)	Telecommunications	United States
402	St. Jude Medical	US standards (GAAP)	Health Care	United States
403	Standard Bank	IFRS	Banks	South Africa
404	Stanley Black & Decker	-	Personal & Household Goods	United States
405	Staples	US standards (GAAP)	Retail	United States
406	Starbucks	US standards (GAAP)	Food & Beverage	United States
407	Starwood Hotels & Resorts	US standards (GAAP)	Travel & Leisure	United States
408	State Street Corp.	US standards (GAAP)	Banks	United States
409	Steelcase	US standards (GAAP)	Personal & Household Goods	United States
410	STMicroelectronics	-	Technology	Switzerland
411	Stockland	IFRS	Real Estate	Australia
412	Stora Enso	IFRS	Basic Resources	Finland
413	Sumitomo Chemical	Local standards	Chemicals	Japan
414	Sumitomo Electric Industries	Local standards	Personal & Household Goods	Japan

continued on following page

Table 1. Continued

Crt. No.	Organization	Accounting Standards	Industry	Country
415	Sumitomo Mitsui Financial Group	Local standards	Banks	Japan
416	SunTrust Banks	US standards (GAAP)	Banks	United States
417	Supervalu	US standards (GAAP)	Retail	United States
418	Surgutneftegas	Local standards	Oil & Gas	Russia
419	Syngenta AG	IFRS	Food & Beverage	Switzerland
420	T. Rowe Price	US standards (GAAP)	Financial Services	United States
421	Taiwan Semiconductor Manufacturing	Local standards	Technology	Taiwan
422	Tata Motors Ltd.	Local standards	Automobiles & Parts	India
423	Tata Steel	Local standards	Basic Resources	India
424	Telecom Italia	-	Telecommunications	Italy
425	Telefónica	IFRS	Telecommunications	Spain
426	Telenor ASA	IFRS	Telecommunications	Norway
427	Tenet Healthcare	-	Health Care	United States
428	Teradata	US standards (GAAP)	Technology	United States
429	Texas Instruments	-	Technology	United States
430	The Crown Estate	-	Real Estate	United Kingdom
431	The Dow Chemical Company	US standards (GAAP)	Chemicals	United States
432	Thermo Fisher Scientific	-	Health Care	United States
433	Thomson Reuters	US standards (GAAP)	Financial Services	Canada
434	Time Warner	US standards (GAAP)	Media	United States
435	TITAN	Local standards	Personal & Household Goods	India
436	TJX	-	Retail	United States
437	TNT	IFRS	Industrial Goods & Services	Netherlands
438	Tokio Marine Holdings	-	Insurance	Japan

continued on following page

Table 1. Continued

Crt. No.	Organization	Accounting Standards	Industry	Country
439	TORONTO-DOM BANK	US standards (GAAP)	Banks	Canada
440	Toshiba	US standards (GAAP)	Personal & Household Goods	Japan
441	Total	IFRS	Oil & Gas	France
442	Total System Services	US standards (GAAP)	Financial Services	United States
443	Toyota Motor	US standards (GAAP)	Automobiles & Parts	Japan
444	Toys "R" Us	NA	Personal & Household Goods	United States
445	Transnet	US standards (GAAP)	Industrial Goods & Services	South Africa
446	Travelers Cos.	-	Insurance	United States
447	Tupperware Brands	-	Personal & Household Goods	United States
448	Turkiye Garanti Bankasi Anonim Sirketi	-	Banks	Turkey
449	Tyco International	-	Personal & Household Goods	Switzerland
450	Tyson Foods	US standards (GAAP)	Food & Beverage	United States
451	UBS	IFRS	Banks	Switzerland
452	UniCredit Group	IFRS	Other	Italy
453	Union Pacific	US standards (GAAP)	Industrial Goods & Services	United States
454	Unisys	US standards (GAAP)	Technology	United States
455	United Continental Holdings	Local standards	Travel & Leisure	United States
456	United Rentals Inc	Local standards	Industrial Goods & Services	United States
457	United Stationers	-	Retail	United States
458	United Technologies	-	Industrial Goods & Services	United States
459	Unitedhealth Group Inc	Local standards	Health Care	United States
460	Universal	US standards (GAAP)	Personal & Household Goods	United States
461	Universal Forest Products	US standards (GAAP)	Basic Resources	United States

continued on following page

Table 1. Continued

Crt. No.	Organization	Accounting Standards	Industry	Country
462	Universal Health Services	US standards (GAAP)	Health Care	United States
463	UPM-Kymmene	-	Basic Resources	Finland
464	Vale	Local standards	Basic Resources	Brazil
465	Valero Energy	US standards (GAAP)	Oil & Gas	United States
466	Vancity	-	Financial Services	Canada
467	Viacom	US standards (GAAP)	Media	United States
468	VISA	US standards (GAAP)	Financial Services	United States
469	Vivendi	IFRS	Media	France
470	Volkswagen	-	Automobiles & Parts	Germany
471	Volvo	IFRS	Automobiles & Parts	Sweden
472	Vornado Realty Trust	-	Real Estate	United States
473	W.W. Grainger	-	Retail	United States
474	Wacker Chemie AG	IFRS	Chemicals	Germany
475	Walgreen	-	Retail	United States
476	WALT DISNEY	-	Media	United States
477	Warner Music Group	US standards (GAAP)	Media	United States
478	WellPoint	-	Health Care	United States
479	Wells Fargo	US standards (GAAP)	Banks	United States
480	Wendy's/Arby's Group	US standards (GAAP)	Food & Beverage	United States
481	Werner Enterprises	-	Industrial Goods & Services	United States
482	WESCO International	US standards (GAAP)	Retail	United States
483	WESTPAC BANKING	IFRS	Financial Services	Australia
484	Weyerhaeuser	US standards (GAAP)	Basic Resources	United States
485	Whirlpool	US standards (GAAP)	Personal & Household Goods	United States

APPENDIX 2: QUESTIONNAIRE ON IR

Figure 1.

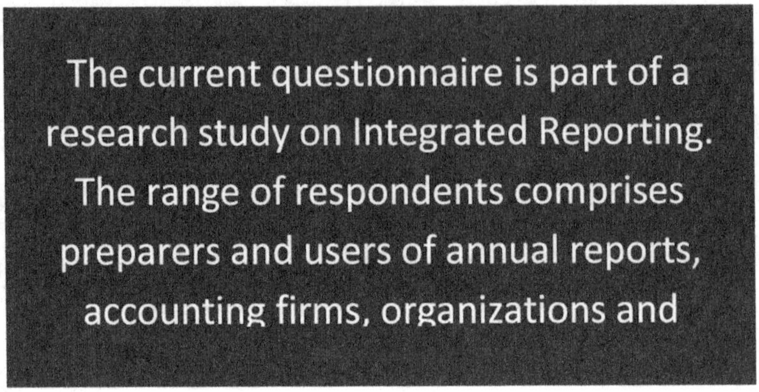

> The current questionnaire is part of a
> research study on Integrated Reporting.
> The range of respondents comprises
> preparers and users of annual reports,
> accounting firms, organizations and

Questionnaire addressing the needs of Integrated Reporting from STAKEHOLDERS' perspective

PhD. Student Ioana DRAGU
Accounting and Audit Department
Faculty of Economic Sciencies and Business Administration, Babes- Bolyai
    University
Romania, Cluj- Napoca

Introduction

Integrated reporting .... It's the way of the future
    First there was sustainability reporting and now there is integrated reporting. And it's set to become the way companies report their annual financial and sustainability information. The aim of an integrated report is to clearly and concisely tell the organization's stakeholders about the company and its strategy and risks, linking its financial and sustainability performance in a way that gives stakeholders a holistic view of the organization and its future prospects.

Financial reporting tells only a part of the story of an organization. Integrated reporting aims to give a holistic view of the organization by putting its performance and strategy in the context of its relevant social and environmental issues. Importantly, integrated reporting includes forward-looking information to allow stakeholders to make a more informed assessment of the future of a company, as well as of how the organization is dealing with its sustainability risks and opportunities.

Ideally, an integrated report should be the organization's primary report and from which all other detailed reports, such as the annual financial statements and sustainability report, flow. A useful analogy is an octopus ... the head is the integrated report and each arm is a detailed report or detailed information set (eg governance information).

King III Code on Governance was one of the first major publications to highlight integrated reporting. It defines an integrated report as "a holistic and integrated representation of the company's performance in terms of both its finance and its sustainability".

The International Integrated Reporting Committee (IIRC) in its discussion paper released in September 2011 defines integrated reporting as: "brings together material information about an organization's strategy, governance, performance and prospects in a way that reflects the commercial, social and environmental context within which it operates. It provides a clear and concise representation of how an organization demonstrates stewardship and how it creates and sustains value. An integrated report should be an organization's primary reporting vehicle."

The IIRC published its Consultation Draft of the International <IR> Framework on 16 April 2013, with a comment deadline of 15 July 2013. The IIRC has released the final version of its <IR> Framework at the end of December 2013.

For more information on the IR topic, please feel free to consult the IIRC website at www.iirc.com

APPENDIX 3

Name (optional) _____
_____

   Phone no. (optional) _____
_____

   E-mail address (optional) _____
_____

   Country _____
_____

   Affiliation _____
_____

   Profession_____
_____

   Position _____
_____

   Category:

☐ Preparer of annual report
☐ User of annual report
☐ Member of accounting profession _____
_____ *(please also indicate the specific profession(s)*
   e.g. FEE, IFAC, CAFR, etc.)
☐ Accounting firm
☐ Organization
Date _____

   We kindly ask you to answer the questions below, by filling in with an 'x' the option you consider most suitable or writing down your own perceptions on certain terms or definitions *(for the open questions)*. Please note that this questionnaire has a general informative purpose and your personal opinion- as expressed here- is not going to be subject for publishing. There is no right or wrong answer- so feel free to choose whatever option you consider from your perspective. All the responses are confidential. In addition, participants can complete the questionnaire anonymously (e.g. you can choose not to write your name on the questionnaire). Your participation in this study is voluntary. If you do not want to participate, please return the questionnaire to the researcher. You also do not have to answer any question that makes you feel uncomfortable.

Thank you for your time.

Q1. I regard my understanding and expertise in this area as:

☐ Slight
☐ Moderate
☐ Average
☐ Good
☐ Very good

Q2. Do you believe that nowadays it is enough for a company to comply with requirements on financial information?

☐ Yes, only financial information is relevant for investors
☐ Yes, non-financial information is not important in decision- making processes
☐ No, because nowadays investors rely on non- financial information also (besides the financial one) when making decisions

Q3. What do you understand by relevant information?

_____

_____

Q4. Why should companies report on non- financial information?

☐ Because of the impact on society and environment
☐ In order to create a "better image" in front of their stakeholders
☐ To enhance reporting transparency
☐ In order to become socially responsible entities
☐ To gain competitive advantage

Q5. Do you consider that current Annual Financial Reports issued by global corporations are too long, too complex, and ambiguous?

☐ Yes
☐ No

If your answer is yes, please provide examples of what information should be excluded or how should the can the Annual financial Reports be simplified.

Q6. Can IR reduce complexity and ambiguity in reporting?

☐ Yes, in some cases - for large companies only, but not for Small Medium Enterprises yes, in all cases;
☐ No

Q7. Are standalone IR reports the only way of practicing integrated reporting?

☐ Yes, because IR means one single report – the Annual Report - that comprises both financial and non- financial informed
☐ No, as corporations can disclose integrated financial and non- financial information in a Corporate Social Responsibility /Environmental / Sustainability Report

Q8. Do you agree that the traditional report can be a predecessor for IR adoption? (By *traditional report* we understand the financial oriented annual report).

☐ **Yes:** traditional reports contain elements of an IR
☐ **No:** the IR is the opposite of a traditional report

Q9. IR is the answer to the current global economic challenges.

☐ I strongly disagree
☐ I disagree
☐ I neither agree nor disagree
☐ I agree
☐ I strongly agree
☐ I am not sure

Please explain your option.

Q10. IR is changing corporate behavior.

☐ Yes, by making companies aware of their impact on people, planet, and profit
☐ Yes, by educating corporations to become more socially responsible in front of society
☐ No, firms will try to use IR for marketing purposes, disclosing only the positive side of their business

Q11. Why do you believe organizations publish these IR?

_____

_____

Q12. Do you think companies are self- motivated to publish these reports or they do it for marketing/image purposes (other reasons- please mention them)?

☐ I believe companies are self – motivated to adopt IR because of the external benefits in terms of reputation and internal advantages of cost reduction

☐ I believe corporations practice IR for marketing/image purposes

☐ other reasons _____

_____

Q13. Which of the following external forces should influence the issuance of IR as an organization reporting behavior?

☐ Political factors
☐ Cultural factors
☐ Economic factors
☐ Social factors
☐ Other factors: _____

_____

Q14. Who should be more interested in reading those reports?

☐ Investors
☐ Analysts
☐ Creditors
☐ NGOs/ environmentalists/ other non-for profit organizations
☐ Governments
☐ Other stakeholders: _____

_____

Q15. The IIRC framework is developed on a set of components (elements): organizational overview and business model; operating context, including risks and opportunities; strategic objectives and strategies to achieve those objectives; governance and remuneration; performance; future outlook. Which elements should be excluded from the framework and why?

_____

_____

Q16. What new elements should be added to the framework and why?

_____

_____

Q17. The IIRC framework contains also a set of principles: *strategic focus; connectivity of information; future orientation; responsiveness and stakeholder inclusiveness; conciseness, reliability and materiality.* Which principles should be excluded from the framework and why?

_____

_____

Q18 What new principles should be added to the framework and why?

_____

_____

Q19. Do you agree that IR should be investor oriented?

☐ Yes, because investors are the main providers of financial capital;
☐ No, because the other stakeholders should receive equal treatment (and IR is addressed to all stakeholders- all report users are important, not only investors).
☐ This depends on other factors such as the size of the company (cannot be applied to SMEs for example)

Q20. Do you agree that the IR framework should concentrate more on shareholder value (and the regular investor) instead of setting disclosure rules for SRI (Social Responsible Investors)?

☐ Shareholder values and the regular investor should be on the first place
☐ The current reporting needs call for disclosure rules for social responsible investors

Q21. What do you understand by INTEGRATION as a process of the IR?

☐ Combining the Sustainability Report with the Annual Report
☐ Integrating information about the business model, the 6 capitals (financial, human, intellectual, social, relational, natural) and corporate governance
☐ Focus and cohesion regarding corporate communications
☐ Integration between departments and cross-functional communications
☐ Integrated thinking

Q22. Which is the difference between CONNECTIVITY and INTERCONNECTION?

☐ Connectivity means creating links between the business model, values, strategy, performance, financial information, risks, governance and regulatory information, while the interconnection sets up inter-relationships between elements of the business
☐ Firms create connectivity between strategy, KPIs and performance, and interconnection between elements of the same system/subsystem.

Q23. How can companies CONNECT internal and external information?

_____

_____

Q24. The IIRC mentions the importance of *value creation and preservation*: "Integrated Reports should enable providers of financial capital to gain an understanding of how an organization creates and sustains value in the short, medium and long term." What does the VALUE represent?

☐ Economic/social value
☐ KPI's/ financial performance
☐ Other sources of value _____

_____

Q25. In your opinion, which are the outcomes of an IR?

☐ Improved relationship with external stakeholders
☐ Obtaining a better corporate image in front of clients, and society as a whole
☐ Less pollution, efficiency in resource allocation
☐ Corporations' accountability towards planet and people
☐ Complying with the trade-off between people, planet and profit
☐ Deeper understanding on the needs of all stakeholders

Q26. Do you think that the progress so far in IR is creating connections/links between departments and people (internal stakeholders)?

☐ I strongly disagree
☐ I disagree
☐ I neither agree nor disagree
☐ I agree
☐ I strongly agree
☐ I am not sure

Please explain your choice.

Q27. How should information be communicated in IR?

☐ Corporations should disclose as much information as possible to enhance reporting transparency
☐ Certain information should remain confidential because of competitors
☐ Firms should disclose only positive impacts / results
☐ Negative aspects should also be revealed in order to have a transparent reporting scheme.

Q28. Who are the users of an IR?

☐ Investors only
☐ Other external stakeholders, such as _____
    _____

☐ Internal stakeholders (e.g. employees)

Q29. Can IR bring 'rewards' for internal and external stakeholders? (Please give examples of such rewards).

☐ Yes, namely _____
    _____

☐ No

Q30. Who are the beneficiaries of IR?

☐ Employees
☐ Customers
☐ Suppliers
☐ Business partners
☐ Local communities
☐ Legislators, regulators and policy makers
☐ Others (please specify) _____
    _____

Q31. What are the benefits of IR?

☐ Increased efficiency of the reporting process
☐ Improvement in decision- making processes
☐ Reduction of cost as information is readily available, and fewer resources need to be put into research

Q32. What are the limitations of IR?

☐ Having no standards for IR
☐ The costs of preparing these reports: the need for specialists; coordination of financial and non-financial information between departments;
☐ Quantifying human, social or intellectual capitals
☐ Defining what to report, to whom, and why

☐ Restrictions from legislation
☐ Determining material non-financial issues
☐ Companies having to explain their business to someone who has no knowledge of the field
☐ Communicating risks and opportunities within the community, and the value of partnerships
☐ Determining what to include in the report to meet stakeholders' expectations

Q33. In your opinion, a company should disclose information about all 6 of its CAPITALS (financial, human, intellectual, social, relational, natural)?

☐ Yes
☐ No (please mention which capitals are to be excluded) _____

_____

Q34. Could you please rank the capitals according to their importance (from 1->6)?

Financial capital ___
Human capital ___
Intellectual capital ___
Social capital ___
Relational capital ___
Natural capital ___

Q35. What implications can the financial capital have on the other capitals?

_____

_____

Q36. Do you believe that all companies should be held accountable in front of society?

☐ Yes, all corporations have a certain impact on society
☐ No, only some high- impact industries (e.g. chemical/oil and gas, etc.)

Q37. Should the IIRC framework be adapted to each sector? (e.g. banks and insurance companies are less harmful to environment than chemical companies).

☐ I strongly disagree
☐ I disagree
☐ I neither agree nor disagree
☐ I agree
☐ I strongly agree
☐ I am not sure

Please explain your option.

_____

_____

Q38. What information should be material for an IR?

_____

_____

Q39. Integrated Reporting should be:

☐ Mandatory
☐ Voluntary
Please explain your option _____

_____

Q40. Do you believe it is too early to consider the assurance, perhaps via some kind of independent 'audit' report, of IR? _____

_____

Q41. Does the corporate reporting environment need a global STANDARD for IR?

☐ I strongly disagree
☐ I disagree
☐ I neither agree nor disagree
☐ I agree
☐ I strongly agree
☐ I am not sure

   Please explain your option _____
_____

Q42. Which policy makers/professional bodies/members of professional bodies is more suitable for issuing such a standard?

☐ IASB- FASB
☐ GRI
☐ SASB
☐ IIRC
☐ State governments
☐ United Nations
☐ other _____

Q43. Are there any other comments you wish to make?

_____
_____

   Thank you for your valuable time taken to complete this Questionnaire.
   Please return the completed Questionnaire to me using the email address: ioana.dragu@econ.ubbcluj.ro

Related Readings

To continue IGI Global's long-standing tradition of advancing innovation through emerging research, please find below a compiled list of recommended IGI Global book chapters and journal articles in the areas of organizational strategy, integrated reporting, and corporate citizenship. These related readings will provide additional information and guidance to further enrich your knowledge and assist you with your own research.

Abbasian-Naghneh, S., Samiei, M., Felahat, M., & Mahdavi, M. (2014). A New Integrative Approach Based on Balanced Scorecard, Data Envelopment Analysis, and Management Performance to Prioritize Research and Development Projects. In I. Osman, A. Anouze, & A. Emrouznejad (Eds.), *Handbook of Research on Strategic Performance Management and Measurement Using Data Envelopment Analysis* (pp. 324–348). Hershey, PA: IGI Global. doi:10.4018/978-1-4666-4474-8.ch007

Aghayi, N., Beigi, Z. G., Gholami, K., & Lotfi, F. H. (2014). Measuring Performance of Dynamic and Network Structures by SBM Model. In I. Osman, A. Anouze, & A. Emrouznejad (Eds.), *Handbook of Research on Strategic Performance Management and Measurement Using Data Envelopment Analysis* (pp. 527–558). Hershey, PA: IGI Global. doi:10.4018/978-1-4666-4474-8.ch017

Agostino, D., Arnaboldi, M., & Azzone, G. (2016). Performance Measurement in Public Networks: Developing a PMS for Network Actors and Network Managers. In A. Ferreira, G. Azevedo, J. Oliveira, & R. Marques (Eds.), *Global Perspectives on Risk Management and Accounting in the Public Sector* (pp. 298–319). Hershey, PA: IGI Global. doi:10.4018/978-1-4666-9803-1.ch015

Agyei-Mensah, B. K. (2016). Impact of Adopting IFRS in Ghana: Empirical Evidence. In E. Uchenna, M. Nnadi, S. Tanna, & F. Iyoha (Eds.), *Economics and Political Implications of International Financial Reporting Standards* (pp. 191–230). Hershey, PA: IGI Global. doi:10.4018/978-1-4666-9876-5.ch010

Aiello, L., & Gatti, M. (2017). Project Portfolio Management and Organization: An Integrated and Circular Model. In L. Romano (Ed.), *Project Portfolio Management Strategies for Effective Organizational Operations* (pp. 288–309). Hershey, PA: IGI Global. doi:10.4018/978-1-5225-2151-8.ch012

Amaral, A. M., & Araújo, M. (2017). Project Portfolio Selection Using a D.E.A. Approach. In L. Romano (Ed.), *Project Portfolio Management Strategies for Effective Organizational Operations* (pp. 220–244). Hershey, PA: IGI Global. doi:10.4018/978-1-5225-2151-8.ch009

Amone, W. (2015). Global Market Trends. In B. Christiansen (Ed.), *Handbook of Research on Global Business Opportunities* (pp. 37–58). Hershey, PA: IGI Global. doi:10.4018/978-1-4666-6551-4.ch002

Anouze, A. L., & Osman, I. H. (2014). Mismanagement or Mismeasurement: The Application of DEA to Generate Performance Values and Insights from Big Data. In I. Osman, A. Anouze, & A. Emrouznejad (Eds.), *Handbook of Research on Strategic Performance Management and Measurement Using Data Envelopment Analysis* (pp. 276–322). Hershey, PA: IGI Global. doi:10.4018/978-1-4666-4474-8.ch006

Aparo von Flüe, A. (2017). Are You Pondering What I Am Pondering?: Eccentric Consideration on Strategic Management. In L. Romano (Ed.), *Project Portfolio Management Strategies for Effective Organizational Operations* (pp. 81–118). Hershey, PA: IGI Global. doi:10.4018/978-1-5225-2151-8.ch004

Araya-Leandro, C., Caba-Pérez, M. D., & López-Hernandez, A. M. (2016). Modernization of Governmental Accounting Systems: Situation in the Central American Region. In A. Ferreira, G. Azevedo, J. Oliveira, & R. Marques (Eds.), *Global Perspectives on Risk Management and Accounting in the Public Sector* (pp. 90–107). Hershey, PA: IGI Global. doi:10.4018/978-1-4666-9803-1.ch005

Archibald, R. D. (2017). Inter-Relationships between an Enterprise's Strategic Management Process and Its Program/Project Portfolio Management Process. In L. Romano (Ed.), *Project Portfolio Management Strategies for Effective Organizational Operations* (pp. 39–60). Hershey, PA: IGI Global. doi:10.4018/978-1-5225-2151-8.ch002

Asongu, S. A. (2016). Rational Asymmetric Development: Transfer Mispricing and Sub-Saharan Africa's Extreme Poverty Tragedy. In E. Uchenna, M. Nnadi, S. Tanna, & F. Iyoha (Eds.), *Economics and Political Implications of International Financial Reporting Standards* (pp. 282–302). Hershey, PA: IGI Global. doi:10.4018/978-1-4666-9876-5.ch014

Baporikar, N. (2015). Effect of National Culture on Development of International Business in the Sultanate of Oman. In B. Christiansen (Ed.), *Handbook of Research on Global Business Opportunities* (pp. 268–288). Hershey, PA: IGI Global. doi:10.4018/978-1-4666-6551-4.ch013

Baporikar, N. (2017). Corporate Leadership and Sustainability. In Z. Fields (Ed.), *Collective Creativity for Responsible and Sustainable Business Practice* (pp. 160–179). Hershey, PA: IGI Global. doi:10.4018/978-1-5225-1823-5.ch009

Baporikar, N. (2017). IT Strategic Planning through CSF Approach in Modern Organizations. In C. Howard & K. Hargiss (Eds.), *Strategic Information Systems and Technologies in Modern Organizations* (pp. 1–20). Hershey, PA: IGI Global. doi:10.4018/978-1-5225-1680-4.ch001

Baraibar-Diez, E., Odriozola, M. D., & Sánchez, J. L. (2017). Storytelling about CSR: Engaging Stakeholders through Storytelling about CSR. In M. Camilleri (Ed.), *CSR 2.0 and the New Era of Corporate Citizenship* (pp. 209–230). Hershey, PA: IGI Global. doi:10.4018/978-1-5225-1842-6.ch011

Baruchello, G. (2017). The Collective Creation of Civil Commons: The Life-Ground of Business Practice. In Z. Fields (Ed.), *Collective Creativity for Responsible and Sustainable Business Practice* (pp. 121–139). Hershey, PA: IGI Global. doi:10.4018/978-1-5225-1823-5.ch007

Beachcroft-Shaw, H., & Ellis, D. (2017). Social Marketing to Achieve Sustainability. In Z. Fields (Ed.), *Collective Creativity for Responsible and Sustainable Business Practice* (pp. 296–314). Hershey, PA: IGI Global. doi:10.4018/978-1-5225-1823-5.ch016

Beachcroft-Shaw, H., & Ellis, D. (2017). Using Successful Cases to Promote Environmental Sustainability: A Social Marketing Approach. In Z. Fields (Ed.), *Collective Creativity for Responsible and Sustainable Business Practice* (pp. 278–295). Hershey, PA: IGI Global. doi:10.4018/978-1-5225-1823-5.ch015

Ben Rejeb, W. (2017). Empirical Evidence on Corporate Governance Impact on CSR Disclosure in Developing Economies: The Tunisian and Egyptian Contexts. In D. Jamali (Ed.), *Comparative Perspectives on Global Corporate Social Responsibility* (pp. 116–137). Hershey, PA: IGI Global. doi:10.4018/978-1-5225-0720-8.ch006

Berberich, R. (2017). Creating Shared Value and Increasing Project Success by Stakeholder Collaboration: A Case in European Manufacturing. In M. Camilleri (Ed.), *CSR 2.0 and the New Era of Corporate Citizenship* (pp. 101–122). Hershey, PA: IGI Global. doi:10.4018/978-1-5225-1842-6.ch006

Bertoni, M., De Rosa, B., Grisi, G., & Rebelli, A. (2015). Linking Cost Control to Cost Management in Healthcare Services: An Analysis of Three Case Studies. In B. Christiansen (Ed.), *Handbook of Research on Global Business Opportunities* (pp. 432–468). Hershey, PA: IGI Global. doi:10.4018/978-1-4666-6551-4.ch021

Boachie, C. (2016). The Effect of International Financial Reporting Standards Adoption on Foreign Direct Investment and the Economy. In E. Uchenna, M. Nnadi, S. Tanna, & F. Iyoha (Eds.), *Economics and Political Implications of International Financial Reporting Standards* (pp. 342–361). Hershey, PA: IGI Global. doi:10.4018/978-1-4666-9876-5.ch017

Boga, S., & Efeoğlu, I. E. (2015). A Case Study on Cross-Cultural Differences: A Failure Story. In B. Christiansen (Ed.), *Handbook of Research on Global Business Opportunities* (pp. 492–531). Hershey, PA: IGI Global. doi:10.4018/978-1-4666-6551-4.ch023

Bortoluzzi, G., de Luca, P., Venier, F., & Balboni, B. (2015). Innovation Scope and the Performance of the Firm: Empirical Evidence from an Italian Wine Cluster. In B. Christiansen (Ed.), *Handbook of Research on Global Business Opportunities* (pp. 551–568). Hershey, PA: IGI Global. doi:10.4018/978-1-4666-6551-4.ch025

Breuer, W., Quinten, B., & Salzmann, A. J. (2015). Bank vs. Bond Finance: A Cultural View of Corporate Debt Financing. In B. Christiansen (Ed.), *Handbook of Research on Global Business Opportunities* (pp. 289–315). Hershey, PA: IGI Global. doi:10.4018/978-1-4666-6551-4.ch014

Bruno, C., & Erbetta, F. (2014). Benchmarking Regulators: A Data Envelopment Analysis of Italian Water Authorities' Performance. In I. Osman, A. Anouze, & A. Emrouznejad (Eds.), *Handbook of Research on Strategic Performance Management and Measurement Using Data Envelopment Analysis* (pp. 388–406). Hershey, PA: IGI Global. doi:10.4018/978-1-4666-4474-8.ch010

Bucero, A. (2017). Linking Organization's Strategy and Strategic Planning with Portfolio Management. In L. Romano (Ed.), *Project Portfolio Management Strategies for Effective Organizational Operations* (pp. 61–80). Hershey, PA: IGI Global. doi:10.4018/978-1-5225-2151-8.ch003

Camilleri, M. A. (2017). The Corporate Sustainability and Responsibility Proposition: A Review and Appraisal. In M. Camilleri (Ed.), *CSR 2.0 and the New Era of Corporate Citizenship* (pp. 1–16). Hershey, PA: IGI Global. doi:10.4018/978-1-5225-1842-6.ch001

Carini, C., & Teodori, C. (2016). Potential Uses and Usefulness of Italian Local Government Consolidated Financial Reporting: The Case of the Town Council of Brescia. In A. Ferreira, G. Azevedo, J. Oliveira, & R. Marques (Eds.), *Global Perspectives on Risk Management and Accounting in the Public Sector* (pp. 68–89). Hershey, PA: IGI Global. doi:10.4018/978-1-4666-9803-1.ch004

Carter, M., & McNulty, Y. (2015). International School Teachers' Professional Development in Response to the Needs of Third Culture Kids in the Classroom. In B. Christiansen (Ed.), *Handbook of Research on Global Business Opportunities* (pp. 367–389). Hershey, PA: IGI Global. doi:10.4018/978-1-4666-6551-4.ch017

Chandan, H. C. (2015). Corruption, Business Climate, and Economic Growth. In B. Christiansen (Ed.), *Handbook of Research on Global Business Opportunities* (pp. 469–491). Hershey, PA: IGI Global. doi:10.4018/978-1-4666-6551-4.ch022

Charles, V., Kumar, M., & Charles, I. K. (2014). The Performance of Printed Circuit Boards in the Presence of Production Errors: A Comparative Analysis Using Various DEA Models. In I. Osman, A. Anouze, & A. Emrouznejad (Eds.), *Handbook of Research on Strategic Performance Management and Measurement Using Data Envelopment Analysis* (pp. 487–509). Hershey, PA: IGI Global. doi:10.4018/978-1-4666-4474-8.ch015

Coste, A. I., & Tiron-Tudor, A. (2016). Performance Measurement Perceptions in Romanian Higher Education. In A. Ferreira, G. Azevedo, J. Oliveira, & R. Marques (Eds.), *Global Perspectives on Risk Management and Accounting in the Public Sector* (pp. 346–365). Hershey, PA: IGI Global. doi:10.4018/978-1-4666-9803-1.ch017

Couto, M. C., & Ferreira, A. D. (2016). The Importance of Accountability Practices in the Public Sector: Literature Review. In A. Ferreira, G. Azevedo, J. Oliveira, & R. Marques (Eds.), *Global Perspectives on Risk Management and Accounting in the Public Sector* (pp. 188–201). Hershey, PA: IGI Global. doi:10.4018/978-1-4666-9803-1.ch010

Cuadrado-Ballesteros, B., García-Sánchez, I. M., & Martínez-Ferrero, J. (2016). Commercialization of Local Public Services. In A. Ferreira, G. Azevedo, J. Oliveira, & R. Marques (Eds.), *Global Perspectives on Risk Management and Accounting in the Public Sector* (pp. 132–150). Hershey, PA: IGI Global. doi:10.4018/978-1-4666-9803-1.ch007

Cuadrado-Ballesteros, B., Mordán, N., & Frías-Aceituno, J. V. (2016). Transparency as a Determinant of Local Financial Condition. In A. Ferreira, G. Azevedo, J. Oliveira, & R. Marques (Eds.), *Global Perspectives on Risk Management and Accounting in the Public Sector* (pp. 202–225). Hershey, PA: IGI Global. doi:10.4018/978-1-4666-9803-1.ch011

Cunha, A., Ferreira, A. D., & Fernandes, M. J. (2016). The Influence of Accounting Information in the Re-Election of the Mayors in Portugal. In A. Ferreira, G. Azevedo, J. Oliveira, & R. Marques (Eds.), *Global Perspectives on Risk Management and Accounting in the Public Sector* (pp. 108–131). Hershey, PA: IGI Global. doi:10.4018/978-1-4666-9803-1.ch006

Das, R. (2015). Do Nonperforming Assets Alone Determine Bank Performance? In B. Christiansen (Ed.), *Handbook of Research on Global Business Opportunities* (pp. 532–550). Hershey, PA: IGI Global. doi:10.4018/978-1-4666-6551-4.ch024

Datta, N. (2014). Dynamic Evaluation of Indian Commercial Banking Sector: A Bank-Level Growth Frontier Approach. In I. Osman, A. Anouze, & A. Emrouznejad (Eds.), *Handbook of Research on Strategic Performance Management and Measurement Using Data Envelopment Analysis* (pp. 600–615). Hershey, PA: IGI Global. doi:10.4018/978-1-4666-4474-8.ch020

Davidson, D. K., & Yin, J. (2017). Corporate Social Responsibility (CSR) in China: A Contextual Exploration. In D. Jamali (Ed.), *Comparative Perspectives on Global Corporate Social Responsibility* (pp. 28–48). Hershey, PA: IGI Global. doi:10.4018/978-1-5225-0720-8.ch002

Davutyan, N., & Bilsel, M. (2014). Efficiency of Turkish Provincial General Hospitals with Mortality as Undesirable Output. In I. Osman, A. Anouze, & A. Emrouznejad (Eds.), *Handbook of Research on Strategic Performance Management and Measurement Using Data Envelopment Analysis* (pp. 426–436). Hershey, PA: IGI Global. doi:10.4018/978-1-4666-4474-8.ch012

de Burgh-Woodman, H., Bressan, A., & Torrisi, A. (2017). An Evaluation of the State of the CSR Field in Australia: Perspectives from the Banking and Mining Sectors. In D. Jamali (Ed.), *Comparative Perspectives on Global Corporate Social Responsibility* (pp. 138–164). Hershey, PA: IGI Global. doi:10.4018/978-1-5225-0720-8.ch007

Del Chiappa, G., Pinna, M., & Atzeni, M. (2017). Barriers to Responsible Tourist Behaviour: A Cluster Analysis in the Context of Italy. In M. Camilleri (Ed.), *CSR 2.0 and the New Era of Corporate Citizenship* (pp. 290–308). Hershey, PA: IGI Global. doi:10.4018/978-1-5225-1842-6.ch015

Devereux, M. T., & Gallarza, M. G. (2017). Social Value Co-Creation: Insights from Consumers, Employees, and Managers. In M. Camilleri (Ed.), *CSR 2.0 and the New Era of Corporate Citizenship* (pp. 76–100). Hershey, PA: IGI Global. doi:10.4018/978-1-5225-1842-6.ch005

Dikeç, A., Kane, V., & Çapar, N. (2017). Cross-Country and Cross-Sector CSR Variations: A Comparative Analysis of CSR Reporting in the U.S., South Korea, and Turkey. In D. Jamali (Ed.), *Comparative Perspectives on Global Corporate Social Responsibility* (pp. 69–95). Hershey, PA: IGI Global. doi:10.4018/978-1-5225-0720-8.ch004

Efeoğlu, I. E., & Christiansen, B. (2015). Turkey: A Rising CIVETS Star? In B. Christiansen (Ed.), *Handbook of Research on Global Business Opportunities* (pp. 59–70). Hershey, PA: IGI Global. doi:10.4018/978-1-4666-6551-4.ch003

Efeoğlu, I. E., & Sanal, M. (2015). The Effects of Work-Family Conflict on Job Stress, Job Satisfaction, and Organizational Commitment: A Study in Turkish Pharmaceutical Industry. In B. Christiansen (Ed.), *Handbook of Research on Global Business Opportunities* (pp. 213–228). Hershey, PA: IGI Global. doi:10.4018/978-1-4666-6551-4.ch010

Eken, M. H., & Kale, S. (2014). Bank Branch Efficiency with DEA. In I. Osman, A. Anouze, & A. Emrouznejad (Eds.), *Handbook of Research on Strategic Performance Management and Measurement Using Data Envelopment Analysis* (pp. 626–667). Hershey, PA: IGI Global. doi:10.4018/978-1-4666-4474-8.ch022

El-Firjani, E. R., & Faraj, S. M. (2016). International Accounting Standards: Adoption, Implementation and Challenges. In E. Uchenna, M. Nnadi, S. Tanna, & F. Iyoha (Eds.), *Economics and Political Implications of International Financial Reporting Standards* (pp. 231–250). Hershey, PA: IGI Global. doi:10.4018/978-1-4666-9876-5.ch011

Elicegui-Reyes, J. I., Barrena-Martínez, J., & Romero-Fernández, P. M. (2017). Emotional Capital and Sustainability in Family Businesses: Human Resource Management Perspective and Sustainability. In M. Camilleri (Ed.), *CSR 2.0 and the New Era of Corporate Citizenship* (pp. 231–250). Hershey, PA: IGI Global. doi:10.4018/978-1-5225-1842-6.ch012

Emrouznejad, A., & Cabanda, E. (2014). Introduction to Data Envelopment Analysis and its Applications. In I. Osman, A. Anouze, & A. Emrouznejad (Eds.), *Handbook of Research on Strategic Performance Management and Measurement Using Data Envelopment Analysis* (pp. 235–255). Hershey, PA: IGI Global. doi:10.4018/978-1-4666-4474-8.ch004

Emrouznejad, A., & Thanassoulis, E. (2014). Introduction to Performance Improvement Management Software (PIM-DEA). In I. Osman, A. Anouze, & A. Emrouznejad (Eds.), *Handbook of Research on Strategic Performance Management and Measurement Using Data Envelopment Analysis* (pp. 256–275). Hershey, PA: IGI Global. doi:10.4018/978-1-4666-4474-8.ch005

Ertek, G., Sevinç, M., Ulus, F., Köse, Ö., & Şahin, G. (2014). A New Framework for Industrial Benchmarking. In I. Osman, A. Anouze, & A. Emrouznejad (Eds.), *Handbook of Research on Strategic Performance Management and Measurement Using Data Envelopment Analysis* (pp. 510–526). Hershey, PA: IGI Global. doi:10.4018/978-1-4666-4474-8.ch016

Ertek, G., Tokdil, B., Günaydın, İ., & Göğüş, A. (2014). Benchmarking Competitiveness of Top 100 U.S. Universities. In I. Osman, A. Anouze, & A. Emrouznejad (Eds.), *Handbook of Research on Strategic Performance Management and Measurement Using Data Envelopment Analysis* (pp. 407–425). Hershey, PA: IGI Global. doi:10.4018/978-1-4666-4474-8.ch011

Falavigna, G., Manello, A., & Pavone, S. (2014). Productivity and Public Funds: A Directional Distance Function Approach Applied to the Italian Agricultural Sector. In I. Osman, A. Anouze, & A. Emrouznejad (Eds.), *Handbook of Research on Strategic Performance Management and Measurement Using Data Envelopment Analysis* (pp. 467–485). Hershey, PA: IGI Global. doi:10.4018/978-1-4666-4474-8.ch014

Fernando, Y., Shaharudin, M. S., & Xin, W. W. (2015). Eco-Innovation Enablers and Typology in Green Furniture Manufacturing. In B. Christiansen (Ed.), *Handbook of Research on Global Business Opportunities* (pp. 416–431). Hershey, PA: IGI Global. doi:10.4018/978-1-4666-6551-4.ch020

Fields, Z., & Atiku, S. O. (2017). Collective Green Creativity and Eco-Innovation as Key Drivers of Sustainable Business Solutions in Organizations. In Z. Fields (Ed.), *Collective Creativity for Responsible and Sustainable Business Practice* (pp. 1–25). Hershey, PA: IGI Global. doi:10.4018/978-1-5225-1823-5.ch001

García de Leaniz, P. M., & Gómez-López, R. (2017). Responsible Management in the CSR 2.0 Era. In M. Camilleri (Ed.), *CSR 2.0 and the New Era of Corporate Citizenship* (pp. 37–54). Hershey, PA: IGI Global. doi:10.4018/978-1-5225-1842-6.ch003

Gomes, P., Camões, S. M., & Carvalho, J. (2016). Determinants of the Design and Use of PMS in Portuguese Government Agencies: A Complementary Theoretical Approach. In A. Ferreira, G. Azevedo, J. Oliveira, & R. Marques (Eds.), *Global Perspectives on Risk Management and Accounting in the Public Sector* (pp. 320–345). Hershey, PA: IGI Global. doi:10.4018/978-1-4666-9803-1.ch016

Grabiński, K., Kędzior, M., & Krasodomska, J. (2016). IFRS Adoption in Poland in the Light of Empirical Research. In E. Uchenna, M. Nnadi, S. Tanna, & F. Iyoha (Eds.), *Economics and Political Implications of International Financial Reporting Standards* (pp. 144–168). Hershey, PA: IGI Global. doi:10.4018/978-1-4666-9876-5.ch008

Grecco, M. C., & Geron, C. M. (2016). The Brazilian Case of IFRS Adoption: The Impacts and the New Perspectives. In E. Uchenna, M. Nnadi, S. Tanna, & F. Iyoha (Eds.), *Economics and Political Implications of International Financial Reporting Standards* (pp. 303–318). Hershey, PA: IGI Global. doi:10.4018/978-1-4666-9876-5.ch015

Gul, M. C., & Kaytaz, M. (2017). CSR and Social Marketing as Enablers of Recovery after the Global Recession: The Turkish Banking Industry. In M. Camilleri (Ed.), *CSR 2.0 and the New Era of Corporate Citizenship* (pp. 274–289). Hershey, PA: IGI Global. doi:10.4018/978-1-5225-1842-6.ch014

Gumz, J. (2017). Managing Change: Strategies and Tactics to Review the Portfolio. In L. Romano (Ed.), *Project Portfolio Management Strategies for Effective Organizational Operations* (pp. 334–357). Hershey, PA: IGI Global. doi:10.4018/978-1-5225-2151-8.ch014

Hack-Polay, D., & Qiu, H. (2017). Doing Good Doing Well: Discussion of CSR in the Pulp and Paper Industry in the Asian Context. In D. Jamali (Ed.), *Comparative Perspectives on Global Corporate Social Responsibility* (pp. 226–240). Hershey, PA: IGI Global. doi:10.4018/978-1-5225-0720-8.ch011

Haro-de-Rosario, A., del Mar Gálvez-Rodríguez, M., & Caba-Pérez, M. D. (2017). Determinants of Corporate Social Responsibility Disclosure in Latin American Companies: An Analysis of the Oil and Gas Sector. In D. Jamali (Ed.), *Comparative Perspectives on Global Corporate Social Responsibility* (pp. 165–184). Hershey, PA: IGI Global. doi:10.4018/978-1-5225-0720-8.ch008

Hassan, A., & Lund-Thomsen, P. (2017). Multi-Stakeholder Initiatives and Corporate Social Responsibility in Global Value Chains: Towards an Analytical Framework and a Methodology. In D. Jamali (Ed.), *Comparative Perspectives on Global Corporate Social Responsibility* (pp. 241–257). Hershey, PA: IGI Global. doi:10.4018/978-1-5225-0720-8.ch012

Holland, P. G., & Alakavuklar, O. N. (2017). Corporate Social Responsibility (CSR) Reporting and Seeking Legitimacy of Māori Communities: A Case from Aotearoa New Zealand Energy Sector. In M. Camilleri (Ed.), *CSR 2.0 and the New Era of Corporate Citizenship* (pp. 123–146). Hershey, PA: IGI Global. doi:10.4018/978-1-5225-1842-6.ch007

Hunter, M. G. (2015). Entrepreneurs' Contributions to Small Business: A Comparison of Success and Failure. In B. Christiansen (Ed.), *Handbook of Research on Global Business Opportunities* (pp. 168–198). Hershey, PA: IGI Global. doi:10.4018/978-1-4666-6551-4.ch008

Igbinakhase, I. (2017). Responsible and Sustainable Management Practices in Developing and Developed Business Environments. In Z. Fields (Ed.), *Collective Creativity for Responsible and Sustainable Business Practice* (pp. 180–207). Hershey, PA: IGI Global. doi:10.4018/978-1-5225-1823-5.ch010

Issa, T., & Pick, D. (2017). Teaching Business Ethics Post GFC: A Corporate Social Responsibility of Universities. In D. Jamali (Ed.), *Comparative Perspectives on Global Corporate Social Responsibility* (pp. 290–307). Hershey, PA: IGI Global. doi:10.4018/978-1-5225-0720-8.ch015

Jindrichovska, I., & Kubickova, D. (2016). Economic and Political Implications of IFRS Adoption in the Czech Republic. In E. Uchenna, M. Nnadi, S. Tanna, & F. Iyoha (Eds.), *Economics and Political Implications of International Financial Reporting Standards* (pp. 105–133). Hershey, PA: IGI Global. doi:10.4018/978-1-4666-9876-5.ch006

Kaplan, J., & Montiel, I. (2017). East vs. West Approaches to Reporting Corporate Sustainability Strategies to the World: Corporate Sustainability Reporting: East vs. West. In D. Jamali (Ed.), *Comparative Perspectives on Global Corporate Social Responsibility* (pp. 49–68). Hershey, PA: IGI Global. doi:10.4018/978-1-5225-0720-8.ch003

Kesic, D. (2015). Research of Strategic Global Development Trends and Competitiveness in the World Pharmaceutical Industry. In B. Christiansen (Ed.), *Handbook of Research on Global Business Opportunities* (pp. 390–401). Hershey, PA: IGI Global. doi:10.4018/978-1-4666-6551-4.ch018

Kittilaksanawong, W., & Dai, W. (2015). Globalization of Latecomer Asian Multinationals and Theory of Multinational Enterprise. In B. Christiansen (Ed.), *Handbook of Research on Global Business Opportunities* (pp. 103–130). Hershey, PA: IGI Global. doi:10.4018/978-1-4666-6551-4.ch005

Krivonozhko, V. E., Piskunov, A. A., Lychev, A. V., & Ivasechko, M. A. (2014). Models and Methods for Decision Making Support in the Negotiation Process. In I. Osman, A. Anouze, & A. Emrouznejad (Eds.), *Handbook of Research on Strategic Performance Management and Measurement Using Data Envelopment Analysis* (pp. 349–371). Hershey, PA: IGI Global. doi:10.4018/978-1-4666-4474-8.ch008

Le, N., Li, X., & Yukhanaev, A. (2015). Locational Determinants of Foreign Direct Investment in the Vietnamese Economy. In B. Christiansen (Ed.), *Handbook of Research on Global Business Opportunities* (pp. 1–36). Hershey, PA: IGI Global. doi:10.4018/978-1-4666-6551-4.ch001

Levin, G., & Pitotti, N. (2017). Program and Portfolio Management Relationship and Support. In L. Romano (Ed.), *Project Portfolio Management Strategies for Effective Organizational Operations* (pp. 310–333). Hershey, PA: IGI Global. doi:10.4018/978-1-5225-2151-8.ch013

Lokuwaduge, C. S. (2016). Exploring the New Public Management (NPM)-Based Reforms in the Public Sector Accounting: A Sri Lankan Study. In A. Ferreira, G. Azevedo, J. Oliveira, & R. Marques (Eds.), *Global Perspectives on Risk Management and Accounting in the Public Sector* (pp. 49–67). Hershey, PA: IGI Global. doi:10.4018/978-1-4666-9803-1.ch003

Madawaki, A. (2016). Adoption of International Financial Reporting Standards and the Changing Accounting Environment in Nigeria. In E. Uchenna, M. Nnadi, S. Tanna, & F. Iyoha (Eds.), *Economics and Political Implications of International Financial Reporting Standards* (pp. 1–26). Hershey, PA: IGI Global. doi:10.4018/978-1-4666-9876-5.ch001

Magalhães, F. R., & Santos, C. (2016). Online Financial Transparency: Local Governments of the MERCOSUR Member Countries. In A. Ferreira, G. Azevedo, J. Oliveira, & R. Marques (Eds.), *Global Perspectives on Risk Management and Accounting in the Public Sector* (pp. 252–273). Hershey, PA: IGI Global. doi:10.4018/978-1-4666-9803-1.ch013

Martinelli-Lee, T., & Duncan, K. B. (2015). International Joint Ventures at the Crossroads: Building Leadership Bridges. In B. Christiansen (Ed.), *Handbook of Research on Global Business Opportunities* (pp. 150–167). Hershey, PA: IGI Global. doi:10.4018/978-1-4666-6551-4.ch007

Martinelli-Lee, T., & Kahan, J. (2015). Waiting to Exhale: Marketing of E-Cigarettes. In B. Christiansen (Ed.), *Handbook of Research on Global Business Opportunities* (pp. 402–415). Hershey, PA: IGI Global. doi:10.4018/978-1-4666-6551-4.ch019

Mendes, H. C., Santos, C., Ferreira, A. D., Marques, R. P., Azevedo, G. M., & Oliveira, J. D. (2016). Local Authorities and the Disclosure of Financial Information via the Internet: The Portuguese Case. In A. Ferreira, G. Azevedo, J. Oliveira, & R. Marques (Eds.), *Global Perspectives on Risk Management and Accounting in the Public Sector* (pp. 274–297). Hershey, PA: IGI Global. doi:10.4018/978-1-4666-9803-1.ch014

Mokoqama, M., & Fields, Z. (2017). Principles of Responsible Management Education (PRME): Call for Responsible Management Education. In Z. Fields (Ed.), *Collective Creativity for Responsible and Sustainable Business Practice* (pp. 229–241). Hershey, PA: IGI Global. doi:10.4018/978-1-5225-1823-5.ch012

Mulwa, R. (2014). Non-Parametric Estimation of Environmental Efficiency Using Data Envelopment Analysis and Free Disposable Hull. In I. Osman, A. Anouze, & A. Emrouznejad (Eds.), *Handbook of Research on Strategic Performance Management and Measurement Using Data Envelopment Analysis* (pp. 437–466). Hershey, PA: IGI Global. doi:10.4018/978-1-4666-4474-8.ch013

Naidoo, V. (2017). The Use of Social Media and Online Petitions to Achieve Collective Change for a Sustainable Future. In Z. Fields (Ed.), *Collective Creativity for Responsible and Sustainable Business Practice* (pp. 261–277). Hershey, PA: IGI Global. doi:10.4018/978-1-5225-1823-5.ch014

Nesbitt, R., & Kotb, A. (2016). Governance in NHS Foundation Trusts: Insights from Company Secretaries. In A. Ferreira, G. Azevedo, J. Oliveira, & R. Marques (Eds.), *Global Perspectives on Risk Management and Accounting in the Public Sector* (pp. 167–187). Hershey, PA: IGI Global. doi:10.4018/978-1-4666-9803-1.ch009

Nnadi, M., & Tanna, S. (2016). IFRS Adoption in the EU and the Challenge of Nomenclature Evidence from the UK, France, and Germany. In E. Uchenna, M. Nnadi, S. Tanna, & F. Iyoha (Eds.), *Economics and Political Implications of International Financial Reporting Standards* (pp. 134–143). Hershey, PA: IGI Global. doi:10.4018/978-1-4666-9876-5.ch007

Nonino, F. (2017). Project Selection Frameworks and Methodologies for Reducing Risks in Project Portfolio Management. In L. Romano (Ed.), *Project Portfolio Management Strategies for Effective Organizational Operations* (pp. 245–263). Hershey, PA: IGI Global. doi:10.4018/978-1-5225-2151-8.ch010

Odia, J. O. (2016). The Determinants and Financial Statement Effects of IFRS Adoption in Nigeria. In E. Uchenna, M. Nnadi, S. Tanna, & F. Iyoha (Eds.), *Economics and Political Implications of International Financial Reporting Standards* (pp. 319–341). Hershey, PA: IGI Global. doi:10.4018/978-1-4666-9876-5.ch016

Ogunsanya, O. (2017). Connecting the Dots: Bisociation, Collective Creativity, and Sustainable Business. In Z. Fields (Ed.), *Collective Creativity for Responsible and Sustainable Business Practice* (pp. 26–41). Hershey, PA: IGI Global. doi:10.4018/978-1-5225-1823-5.ch002

Ojo, M. (2016). Corporate Social Responsibility and Foreign Direct Investment: Engaging Innovation, Auditors, and Stakeholders in Corporate Social Responsibility. In M. Ojo (Ed.), *Analyzing the Relationship between Corporate Social Responsibility and Foreign Direct Investment* (pp. 49–63). Hershey, PA: IGI Global. doi:10.4018/978-1-5225-0305-7.ch005

Olson, B. (2017). Optimizing Portfolio Value through Comprehensive Project Metrics. In L. Romano (Ed.), *Project Portfolio Management Strategies for Effective Organizational Operations* (pp. 178–201). Hershey, PA: IGI Global. doi:10.4018/978-1-5225-2151-8.ch007

Ormin, K. (2016). Are IFRS Adoption Benefits in Developing Countries a Time-Lag?: A Critical Review of the Case of Nigeria. In E. Uchenna, M. Nnadi, S. Tanna, & F. Iyoha (Eds.), *Economics and Political Implications of International Financial Reporting Standards* (pp. 251–265). Hershey, PA: IGI Global. doi:10.4018/978-1-4666-9876-5.ch012

Osman, I. H., & Anouze, A. L. (2014). A Cognitive Analytics Management Framework (CAM-Part 1): SAMAS Components, Leadership, Frontier Performance Growth, and Sustainable Shared Value. In I. Osman, A. Anouze, & A. Emrouznejad (Eds.), *Handbook of Research on Strategic Performance Management and Measurement Using Data Envelopment Analysis* (pp. 1–79). Hershey, PA: IGI Global. doi:10.4018/978-1-4666-4474-8.ch001

Osman, I. H., & Anouze, A. L. (2014). A Cognitive Analytics Management Framework (CAM-Part 2): Societal Needs, Shared-Value Models, Performance Indicators, Big Data, Business Analytics Models and Tools. In I. Osman, A. Anouze, & A. Emrouznejad (Eds.), *Handbook of Research on Strategic Performance Management and Measurement Using Data Envelopment Analysis* (pp. 80–189). Hershey, PA: IGI Global. doi:10.4018/978-1-4666-4474-8.ch002

Osman, I. H., & Anouze, A. L. (2014). A Cognitive Analytics Management Framework (CAM-Part 3): Critical Skills Shortage, Higher Education Trends, Education Value Chain Framework, Government Strategy. In I. Osman, A. Anouze, & A. Emrouznejad (Eds.), *Handbook of Research on Strategic Performance Management and Measurement Using Data Envelopment Analysis* (pp. 190–234). Hershey, PA: IGI Global. doi:10.4018/978-1-4666-4474-8.ch003

Osman, M. N. (2017). Internet-Based Social Reporting in Emerging Economies: Insights from Public Banks in Egypt and the UAE. In D. Jamali (Ed.), *Comparative Perspectives on Global Corporate Social Responsibility* (pp. 96–115). Hershey, PA: IGI Global. doi:10.4018/978-1-5225-0720-8.ch005

Outa, E. R. (2016). Consequences of IFRS Adoption: A Myth or a Reality – Selected Cases of Adoption Effects. In E. Uchenna, M. Nnadi, S. Tanna, & F. Iyoha (Eds.), *Economics and Political Implications of International Financial Reporting Standards* (pp. 47–65). Hershey, PA: IGI Global. doi:10.4018/978-1-4666-9876-5.ch003

Outa, E. R., & Waweru, N. M. (2016). IFRS Convergence and Revisions: Evidence of Accounting Information Quality from East Africa. In E. Uchenna, M. Nnadi, S. Tanna, & F. Iyoha (Eds.), *Economics and Political Implications of International Financial Reporting Standards* (pp. 169–190). Hershey, PA: IGI Global. doi:10.4018/978-1-4666-9876-5.ch009

Ozuem, W., & Thomas, T. (2015). Inside the Small Island Economies: Loyalty Strategies in the Telecommunications Sector. In B. Christiansen (Ed.), *Handbook of Research on Global Business Opportunities* (pp. 316–349). Hershey, PA: IGI Global. doi:10.4018/978-1-4666-6551-4.ch015

Parth, F. R. (2017). Preparing the Organization for Portfolio Management: Overcoming Resistance and Obstacles. In L. Romano (Ed.), *Project Portfolio Management Strategies for Effective Organizational Operations* (pp. 119–152). Hershey, PA: IGI Global. doi:10.4018/978-1-5225-2151-8.ch005

Parth, F. R. (2017). Project Portfolio Management Growth and Operation: Portfolio Management Structure, Operations, Risk, and Growth. In L. Romano (Ed.), *Project Portfolio Management Strategies for Effective Organizational Operations* (pp. 264–287). Hershey, PA: IGI Global. doi:10.4018/978-1-5225-2151-8.ch011

Patrick, H., & Fields, Z. (2017). A Need for Cyber Security Creativity. In Z. Fields (Ed.), *Collective Creativity for Responsible and Sustainable Business Practice* (pp. 42–61). Hershey, PA: IGI Global. doi:10.4018/978-1-5225-1823-5.ch003

Pečarič, M. (2016). The Awareness of Mentality in Public Administration as the Key for the Management of Its Complexity. In A. Ferreira, G. Azevedo, J. Oliveira, & R. Marques (Eds.), *Global Perspectives on Risk Management and Accounting in the Public Sector* (pp. 1–24). Hershey, PA: IGI Global. doi:10.4018/978-1-4666-9803-1.ch001

Pereira de Campos, C. M., Rodrigues, L. L., & Jorge, S. M. (2016). The Role of Management Accounting Systems in Public Hospitals and the Construction of Budgets: A Literature Review. In A. Ferreira, G. Azevedo, J. Oliveira, & R. Marques (Eds.), *Global Perspectives on Risk Management and Accounting in the Public Sector* (pp. 366–389). Hershey, PA: IGI Global. doi:10.4018/978-1-4666-9803-1.ch018

Phan, D. H., Joshi, M., & Mascitelli, B. (2016). Are Vietnamese Accounting Academics and Practitioners Ready for International Financial Reporting Standards (IFRS)? In E. Uchenna, M. Nnadi, S. Tanna, & F. Iyoha (Eds.), *Economics and Political Implications of International Financial Reporting Standards* (pp. 27–46). Hershey, PA: IGI Global. doi:10.4018/978-1-4666-9876-5.ch002

Phan, D. H., Joshi, M., & Mascitelli, B. (2016). International Financial Reporting Standards (IFRS) Adoption in Vietnam: From Isolation to Isomorphism. In E. Uchenna, M. Nnadi, S. Tanna, & F. Iyoha (Eds.), *Economics and Political Implications of International Financial Reporting Standards* (pp. 266–281). Hershey, PA: IGI Global. doi:10.4018/978-1-4666-9876-5.ch013

Pinho, M., & Santos, C. (2016). Plan for Prevention of Risks of Corruption and Related Infractions: The Application of FMEA Methodology. In A. Ferreira, G. Azevedo, J. Oliveira, & R. Marques (Eds.), *Global Perspectives on Risk Management and Accounting in the Public Sector* (pp. 390–412). Hershey, PA: IGI Global. doi:10.4018/978-1-4666-9803-1.ch019

Poveda, A. C. (2014). Corruption, Economic Development, and Insecurity in Colombia. In I. Osman, A. Anouze, & A. Emrouznejad (Eds.), *Handbook of Research on Strategic Performance Management and Measurement Using Data Envelopment Analysis* (pp. 373–387). Hershey, PA: IGI Global. doi:10.4018/978-1-4666-4474-8.ch009

Puaschunder, J. (2017). The Call for Global Responsible Inter-Generational Leadership: The Quest of an Integration of Inter-Generational Equity in Corporate Social Responsibility (CSR) Models. In D. Jamali (Ed.), *Comparative Perspectives on Global Corporate Social Responsibility* (pp. 276–289). Hershey, PA: IGI Global. doi:10.4018/978-1-5225-0720-8.ch014

Radovic, V. M. (2017). Corporate Sustainability and Responsibility and Disaster Risk Reduction: A Serbian Overview. In M. Camilleri (Ed.), *CSR 2.0 and the New Era of Corporate Citizenship* (pp. 147–164). Hershey, PA: IGI Global. doi:10.4018/978-1-5225-1842-6.ch008

Rahdari, A. H. (2017). Fostering Responsible Business: Evidence from Leading Corporate Social Responsibility and Sustainability Networks. In M. Camilleri (Ed.), *CSR 2.0 and the New Era of Corporate Citizenship* (pp. 309–330). Hershey, PA: IGI Global. doi:10.4018/978-1-5225-1842-6.ch016

Raimi, L. (2017). Leveraging CSR as a 'support-aid' for Triple Bottom-Line Development in Nigeria: Evidence from the Telecommunication Industry. In D. Jamali (Ed.), *Comparative Perspectives on Global Corporate Social Responsibility* (pp. 208–225). Hershey, PA: IGI Global. doi:10.4018/978-1-5225-0720-8.ch010

Ray, L., & Felch, H. (2017). Detecting Advanced Persistent Threats in Oracle Databases: Methods and Techniques. In C. Howard & K. Hargiss (Eds.), *Strategic Information Systems and Technologies in Modern Organizations* (pp. 71–89). Hershey, PA: IGI Global. doi:10.4018/978-1-5225-1680-4.ch004

Rinderu, P., Voiculescu, C. I., & Visanescu, D. L. (2016). Risks in Implementing EU-Funded Projects in Romanian Public Higher Education System: Measures for Better Institutional Response. In A. Ferreira, G. Azevedo, J. Oliveira, & R. Marques (Eds.), *Global Perspectives on Risk Management and Accounting in the Public Sector* (pp. 413–441). Hershey, PA: IGI Global. doi:10.4018/978-1-4666-9803-1.ch020

Romano, L. (2017). Adaptive Portfolio Management. In L. Romano (Ed.), *Project Portfolio Management Strategies for Effective Organizational Operations* (pp. 153–177). Hershey, PA: IGI Global. doi:10.4018/978-1-5225-2151-8.ch006

Romano, L. (2017). Portfolio Management as a Step into the Future. In L. Romano (Ed.), *Project Portfolio Management Strategies for Effective Organizational Operations* (pp. 1–38). Hershey, PA: IGI Global. doi:10.4018/978-1-5225-2151-8.ch001

Romano, L., Grimaldi, R., & Colasuonno, F. S. (2017). Demand Management as a Success Factor in Project Portfolio Management. In L. Romano (Ed.), *Project Portfolio Management Strategies for Effective Organizational Operations* (pp. 202–219). Hershey, PA: IGI Global. doi:10.4018/978-1-5225-2151-8.ch008

Rusko, R., Hietanen, L., Kohtakangas, K., Kemppainen-Koivisto, R., Siltavirta, K., & Järvi, T. (2017). Educational and Business Co-Operatives: The Channels for Collective Creativity and Entrepreneurial Teams. In Z. Fields (Ed.), *Collective Creativity for Responsible and Sustainable Business Practice* (pp. 242–259). Hershey, PA: IGI Global. doi:10.4018/978-1-5225-1823-5.ch013

Sá, F., Rocha, Á., & Pérez-Cota, M. (2016). A Literature Review on Quality Models for Online E-Government Services. In A. Ferreira, G. Azevedo, J. Oliveira, & R. Marques (Eds.), *Global Perspectives on Risk Management and Accounting in the Public Sector* (pp. 151–166). Hershey, PA: IGI Global. doi:10.4018/978-1-4666-9803-1.ch008

Sánchez-Fernández, M. D., Cardona, J. R., & Martínez-Fernández, V. (2017). Comparative Perspectives on CSR 2.0 in the Contexts of Galicia and North of Portugal. In M. Camilleri (Ed.), *CSR 2.0 and the New Era of Corporate Citizenship* (pp. 165–186). Hershey, PA: IGI Global. doi:10.4018/978-1-5225-1842-6.ch009

Sarter, E. K. (2017). CSR, Public Spending, and the State: The Use of Public Procurement as a Lever to Foster Social Responsibility. In M. Camilleri (Ed.), *CSR 2.0 and the New Era of Corporate Citizenship* (pp. 55–75). Hershey, PA: IGI Global. doi:10.4018/978-1-5225-1842-6.ch004

Serrano, F. V., Guerrero, L. R., Cheng, G., Zervopoulos, P. D., & Moreno, A. C. (2014). Global Financial Crisis and Bank Productivity in Mexico. In I. Osman, A. Anouze, & A. Emrouznejad (Eds.), *Handbook of Research on Strategic Performance Management and Measurement Using Data Envelopment Analysis* (pp. 581–599). Hershey, PA: IGI Global. doi:10.4018/978-1-4666-4474-8.ch019

Shambaugh, N. (2017). Empowerment of Communities to Address Impossible Problems. In Z. Fields (Ed.), *Collective Creativity for Responsible and Sustainable Business Practice* (pp. 62–81). Hershey, PA: IGI Global. doi:10.4018/978-1-5225-1823-5.ch004

Shankar, A., & Das, R. (2015). Eminent Domain in Argentina, Brazil, and Mexico. In B. Christiansen (Ed.), *Handbook of Research on Global Business Opportunities* (pp. 350–366). Hershey, PA: IGI Global. doi:10.4018/978-1-4666-6551-4.ch016

Shiri, A. T. (2017). The Role of Leadership in Cultivating a Responsible Collective Creative Work Environment. In Z. Fields (Ed.), *Collective Creativity for Responsible and Sustainable Business Practice* (pp. 82–105). Hershey, PA: IGI Global. doi:10.4018/978-1-5225-1823-5.ch005

Sinha, R. P., & Datta, N. (2014). Performance Benchmarking of the Indian Life Insurance Industry: A Unified Approach. In I. Osman, A. Anouze, & A. Emrouznejad (Eds.), *Handbook of Research on Strategic Performance Management and Measurement Using Data Envelopment Analysis* (pp. 616–625). Hershey, PA: IGI Global. doi:10.4018/978-1-4666-4474-8.ch021

Sitnikov, C. S., Bocean, C., & Tudor, S. (2017). Integrating New Visions of Education Models and CSR 2.0 towards University Social Responsibility (USR). In M. Camilleri (Ed.), *CSR 2.0 and the New Era of Corporate Citizenship* (pp. 251–273). Hershey, PA: IGI Global. doi:10.4018/978-1-5225-1842-6.ch013

Sowa, F., & Staples, R. (2016). Public Administration in the Era of Late Neo-Liberalism: Placement Professionals and the NPM Regime. In A. Ferreira, G. Azevedo, J. Oliveira, & R. Marques (Eds.), *Global Perspectives on Risk Management and Accounting in the Public Sector* (pp. 25–48). Hershey, PA: IGI Global. doi:10.4018/978-1-4666-9803-1.ch002

Sraha, G. (2015). Public Policy Makers: Export Promotion Programmes and Global Competitiveness in Sub-Saharan Africa. In B. Christiansen (Ed.), *Handbook of Research on Global Business Opportunities* (pp. 199–212). Hershey, PA: IGI Global. doi:10.4018/978-1-4666-6551-4.ch009

Stainbank, L., & Tauringana, V. (2016). Determinants of and Obstacles to the Adoption of International Financial Reporting Standards in Africa. In E. Uchenna, M. Nnadi, S. Tanna, & F. Iyoha (Eds.), *Economics and Political Implications of International Financial Reporting Standards* (pp. 66–82). Hershey, PA: IGI Global. doi:10.4018/978-1-4666-9876-5.ch004

Taminiau, J., Nyangon, J., Lewis, A. S., & Byrne, J. (2017). Sustainable Business Model Innovation: Using Polycentric and Creative Climate Change Governance. In Z. Fields (Ed.), *Collective Creativity for Responsible and Sustainable Business Practice* (pp. 140–159). Hershey, PA: IGI Global. doi:10.4018/978-1-5225-1823-5.ch008

Tan, B. U. (2017). Responsible Corporate Behaviors: Drivers of Corporate Responsibility. In M. Camilleri (Ed.), *CSR 2.0 and the New Era of Corporate Citizenship* (pp. 17–36). Hershey, PA: IGI Global. doi:10.4018/978-1-5225-1842-6.ch002

Tanrikulu, C., & Gelibolu, L. (2015). Impact of Culture on Service Failures and Service Recoveries. In B. Christiansen (Ed.), *Handbook of Research on Global Business Opportunities* (pp. 229–238). Hershey, PA: IGI Global. doi:10.4018/978-1-4666-6551-4.ch011

Tavares, M. D., & Rodrigues, L. L. (2016). The Determinants of Sustainability Reporting of the Portuguese Public Sector Entities. In A. Ferreira, G. Azevedo, J. Oliveira, & R. Marques (Eds.), *Global Perspectives on Risk Management and Accounting in the Public Sector* (pp. 226–251). Hershey, PA: IGI Global. doi:10.4018/978-1-4666-9803-1.ch012

Tirado-Cordero, I., & Hargiss, K. M. (2017). Exploring Local Interaction Attributes Affecting Leadership Effectiveness on Assignment in Multinational Companies: A Qualitative Phenomenological Study. In C. Howard & K. Hargiss (Eds.), *Strategic Information Systems and Technologies in Modern Organizations* (pp. 37–70). Hershey, PA: IGI Global. doi:10.4018/978-1-5225-1680-4.ch003

Uchenna, E., & Iyoha, F. (2016). IFRS, Foreign Investment, and Prevailing Institutional Structure in Africa. In E. Uchenna, M. Nnadi, S. Tanna, & F. Iyoha (Eds.), *Economics and Political Implications of International Financial Reporting Standards* (pp. 83–104). Hershey, PA: IGI Global. doi:10.4018/978-1-4666-9876-5.ch005

Valcik, N. A. (2017). Using Geospatial Information Systems for Strategic Planning and Institutional Research for Higher Education Institutions. In C. Howard & K. Hargiss (Eds.), *Strategic Information Systems and Technologies in Modern Organizations* (pp. 21–36). Hershey, PA: IGI Global. doi:10.4018/978-1-5225-1680-4.ch002

Van der Westhuizen, T. (2017). A Systemic Approach towards Responsible and Sustainable Economic Development: Entrepreneurship, Systems Theory, and Socio-Economic Momentum. In Z. Fields (Ed.), *Collective Creativity for Responsible and Sustainable Business Practice* (pp. 208–227). Hershey, PA: IGI Global. doi:10.4018/978-1-5225-1823-5.ch011

Van der Westhuizen, T., & Mkhonta, M. (2017). Co-Engagement of Organisational Leadership in Collective Decision-Making: A Case of Public Enterprise. In Z. Fields (Ed.), *Collective Creativity for Responsible and Sustainable Business Practice* (pp. 106–119). Hershey, PA: IGI Global. doi:10.4018/978-1-5225-1823-5.ch006

Vecchi, A., & Brennan, L. (2015). Leveraging Business Model Innovation in the International Space Industry. In B. Christiansen (Ed.), *Handbook of Research on Global Business Opportunities* (pp. 131–149). Hershey, PA: IGI Global. doi:10.4018/978-1-4666-6551-4.ch006

Windsor, D. (2017). Defining Corporate Social Responsibility for Developing and Developed Countries: Comparing Proposed Approaches. In D. Jamali (Ed.), *Comparative Perspectives on Global Corporate Social Responsibility* (pp. 1–27). Hershey, PA: IGI Global. doi:10.4018/978-1-5225-0720-8.ch001

Wolf, R., & Thiel, M. (2017). CSR in China: The Road to New Sustainable Business Models. In D. Jamali (Ed.), *Comparative Perspectives on Global Corporate Social Responsibility* (pp. 258–275). Hershey, PA: IGI Global. doi:10.4018/978-1-5225-0720-8.ch013

Yap, N. T., & Ground, K. E. (2017). Socially Responsible Mining Corporations: Before (or in Addition to) Doing Good, Do No Harm. In D. Jamali (Ed.), *Comparative Perspectives on Global Corporate Social Responsibility* (pp. 185–207). Hershey, PA: IGI Global. doi:10.4018/978-1-5225-0720-8.ch009

Yenilmez, F. (2014). The Efficiency Performance of the Turkish Ceramic Sector in Terms of Revenue and Export: DEA Model. In I. Osman, A. Anouze, & A. Emrouznejad (Eds.), *Handbook of Research on Strategic Performance Management and Measurement Using Data Envelopment Analysis* (pp. 559–579). Hershey, PA: IGI Global. doi:10.4018/978-1-4666-4474-8.ch018

Yukhanaev, A., Nguyen, T., Demirbas, D., & Galvin, P. (2015). International Integration and Corporate Governance Practices in Russia. In B. Christiansen (Ed.), *Handbook of Research on Global Business Opportunities* (pp. 239–267). Hershey, PA: IGI Global. doi:10.4018/978-1-4666-6551-4.ch012

Zebregs, A., & Moratis, L. (2017). Serving the Purpose?: Communicating Self-Serving CSR Motives to Increase Credibility. In M. Camilleri (Ed.), *CSR 2.0 and the New Era of Corporate Citizenship* (pp. 187–208). Hershey, PA: IGI Global. doi:10.4018/978-1-5225-1842-6.ch010

Zuber, C., & Pfohl, H. (2015). Cultural Management for Multinational Enterprises. In B. Christiansen (Ed.), *Handbook of Research on Global Business Opportunities* (pp. 71–102). Hershey, PA: IGI Global. doi:10.4018/978-1-4666-6551-4.ch004

Index

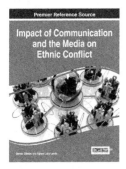

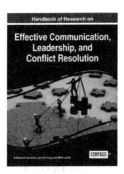

Stay Current on the Latest Emerging Research Developments

Become an IGI Global Reviewer for Authored Book Projects

Premier Reference Source

Emerging GIS Applications for Emergency and Disaster Management

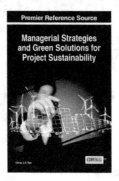

Premier Reference Source

Managerial Strategies and Green Solutions for Project Sustainability

Premier Reference Source

Comparative Approaches to Using R and Python for Statistical Data Analysis

Premier Reference Source

Solutions for High-Touch Communications in a High-Tech World

The overall success of an authored book project is dependent on quality and timely reviews.

In this competitive age of scholarly publishing, constructive and timely feedback significantly decreases the turnaround time of manuscripts from submission to acceptance, allowing the publication and discovery of progressive research at a much more expeditious rate. Several IGI Global authored book projects are currently seeking highly qualified experts in the field to fill vacancies on their respective editorial review boards:

Applications may be sent to:
development@igi-global.com

Applicants must have a doctorate (or an equivalent degree) as well as publishing and reviewing experience. Reviewers are asked to write reviews in a timely, collegial, and constructive manner. All reviewers will begin their role on an ad-hoc basis for a period of one year, and upon successful completion of this term can be considered for full editorial review board status, with the potential for a subsequent promotion to Associate Editor.

If you have a colleague that may be interested in this opportunity, we encourage you to share this information with them.

Printed in the United States
By Bookmasters